WHEN THE CAR
AND THE
CITY COLLIDE

# CARCHITECTURE

JONATHAN BELL

August – London

Birkhäuser –
Publishers for Architecture
Basel·Boston·Berlin

FROM HERE
TO THERE
ALEX S.
MacLEAN

P.10

1.

FROM HERE
TO THERE
ALEX S.
MacLEAN
P.2

MIRROR,
SIGNAL,
MANŒUVRE

BRING YOUR
OWN SPACE
HEATHER
PUTTOCK
P.20

SOME
GARAGES
ANDREW
CROSS
P.24

# CARCHIT

Deutsche Bibliothek Cataloging-in-Publication Data

Carchitecture / ed. by Jonathan Bell.
– Basel ; Boston ; Berlin : Birkhäuser;
London : August, 2001
ISBN 3-7643-6454-8

© 2001 Birkhäuser – Publishers for Architecture, P.O. Box 133, CH-4010 Basel, Switzerland.
Member of the BertelsmannSpringer Publishing Group.
© 2001 August Media Ltd,
116-120 Golden Lane,
London EC1Y 0TL, UK

Printed on acid-free paper produced of chlorine-free pulp.
TCF ∞
Printed in Italy

ISBN 3-7643-6454-8

9 8 7 6 5 4 3 2 1

Author: Jonathan Bell, with additional texts by Liz Bailey, Clare Dowdy, Sandy McCreery, Heather Puttock and Austin Williams.

August
Publishing director: Nick Barley
Art director: Stephen Coates
Project editor: Alex Stetter
Editorial assistant: Ruth Ward
Picture researcher: Heather Vickers
Production coordinated by:
Uwe Kraus GmbH

Publisher's acknowledgements:
Fiona Bradley, Nicole Liniger, Marit Münzberg, Anne Odling-Smee, Anni Scheder-Bieschin, Elisabeth Scheder-Bieschin, Robert Steiger, Veronika Stetter.

Author's acknowledgements:
Alex de Rijke, Catherine Croft.

Special thanks to Alex Adie.


www.birkhauser.ch
www.augustmedia.co.uk
www.carchitecture.net

Opposite: Matté-Trucco's
Fiat Factory at Lingotto,
Turin (1914–26)

# ECTURE

# 1. MIRROR, SIGNAL, MANŒUVRE

We are simultaneously at one with our cars and at odds with the automobile. After over a century of integration and accommodation we are still at an impasse; at once a symbol of liberation and a totem of control, the car is adrift in our affections. Now, we are told, we must shun the automobile, wean ourselves off decades of dependence and return cities to the people, a virgin state unsullied by asphalt and rat runs, pedestrian crossings, road rage and danger.

Yet our experience of the city, and hence our response to architecture, is almost exclusively conducted through the medium of the automobile: the car defines our space whether we are driving, being driven or avoiding being driven over. The car has been an integral part of metropolitan life for so long that it has become part of the urban fabric. A surgical removal of the car will surely endanger the life of the patient.

Through the eyes of the motorist, the city is speed, sensation and movement. Yet the city also represents impotence and powerlessness as traffic frustrates movement and hampers potential. For the pedestrian, the automobile is an element to avoid, a threat yet also a facilitator. In Britain at least, non-drivers are in a significant minority. Some 81% of British men and 59% of women hold a driving license. Despite all our protests against cars and their effects, we love to drive. To condemn the car outright denies most people's everyday experience. A more sophisticated response is needed.

Between 1950 and 1980, the number of cars in the world increased from 50 million to 350 million: there are now an estimated 500 million cars on the planet, with some projections suggesting a billion by 2030. In 2000, America's 230,957,227 passenger vehicles travelled some 4 trillion km. Given operating costs of approximately 33 cents per km, cars are costing their drivers over $1.3 trillion a year, of which $80 billion was fuel and vehicle tax. In addition, the social costs generated by the car – traffic jams, accidents, pollution – have been estimated at nearly $500 billion a year. Though it is cited by big business as an anti-capitalist device to deter economic growth, global warming is a reality, and motorists' complicity, however removed their involvement might appear, will have to be challenged.

To accommodate the explosion of the world's car population, our cities have been continuously scoured, razed and rebuilt. The automobile's influence on our environment – both built and natural – is both undeniable yet also strangely invisible; we are conditioned to the winding expanses of highway, buildings skirted by acres of tarmac and whole swathes of countryside given over to flow and contraflow systems that channel our population from one location to another. According to anti-sprawlist Jane Holtz Kay:

> 'Planning for such sixty-mile-an-hour speeds, designing for wastelands of parking, for corridors of concrete, the architect's work has inevitably become carchitecture. Denying the three-mile-an-hour pace of the walker, the world seen from the porch, the surroundings in all their tender detail at an easy pace, the once close-scaled places have spread into a blur with all the individuality and identity of the freeway.'

Carchitecture is a compound word, one so ambiguous in tone that it could have been coined by either side of the debate. The space created in the automobile's wake is carchitecture; the landscape of the car. To opponents of the dreaded sprawl, the word symbolises all that is reprehensible about off-ramp culture; the ceaseless worship of the rights of the driver over other city dwellers. There is no interaction, just 'pedestrian and vehicular conflicts'. In Britain, especially, carchitecture implies overwhelming ugliness, the word's hybridity bristling like the great saw-toothed edges of our concrete multi-storey car parks. We all know this type of carchitecture, be it parking structures, or the low-lying, wipe-clean folksiness of the motorway service station, the white scar that cleaves the meadows of Twyford Down, or the soaring curves of Britain's truncated, stubby motorway system, where major roads sweep over, under and around each other, choking the countryside with their tangled grey web.

Previous studies of the architecture of the automobile have focused, with very few exceptions, on the heroic engineering feats and structures that enhance the speed and drama of automobile travel, as well as facilitate their production and integration into our towns and cities; the story of the modern factory, multi-storey

Designed by Giacomo Matté-Trucco, the spectacular Fiat Factory at Lingotto, Turin (1914–26) featured a vast spiral ramp leading to the famous roof-top test track, which also formed the final stage of the production line. No longer a factory, the building was renovated by Renzo Piano in the 1990s and now houses an extensive hotel and conference complex. It remains one of the most potent symbols of an age when cars heralded a future of mobility, freedom and wealth.

car park, bypass scheme and modernist city plan. Increasingly unfashionable and controversial, the age of the six-lane solution to traffic congestion is slowly being consigned to planning history, a misguided approach that has resulted in as many problems as it solved. Compare our current negativity with the automotive optimism of the past.

Just a few decades ago, the machine-age visions ushered in by the demands of the car were welcomed. In the minds of the world's most progressive architects, urban architecture *was* carchitecture – the car not only revolutionised city organisation and brought unprecedented freedom, it also provided the urbanist with the best sensation of travelling through the metropolis. The car formed an essential component in the modern architect's strategy to improve and re-build, re-shaping every aspect of the urban environment and the world that spread alongside the flowing new roads.

Planning now and then includes the control and mediation of personal transport, not just the design of roadways for channelling people under, through and around towns, but through the design of the very vehicles themselves. The modernists excelled at this multi-disciplinary approach. Le Corbusier and Frank Lloyd Wright are the best-known exponents of this architectural predilection for amateur mechanics. Each favoured large automobiles, even if their driving ability and technical competence were questionable, and their grand, unbuilt city plans – all massively influential on the post-war reconstructionists – were car-centric in the extreme. Le Corbusier, in his typically evangelical style, proclaimed that it remains to use the motor-car as a challenge to our houses and great buildings, foreseeing the automobile's influence yet little realising that the challenge he proposed was the first shot in a war of attrition.

Today, the emphasis is on control and restriction; urbanism has been undermined by the automobile's relentless infiltration. The countryside too has come under attack, with suburbs – the car's most visible contribution to culture – extending their reach, year on year, long tarmacadam fingers stretching across our green and pleasant land. Half of all urban space is devoted to the automobile, and every minute, three acres of American farmland are lost to tarmac, a total of one and half million acres a year. Although the car is integral to our society, hailed since its invention as a social and economic miracle, our cities are now choked by traffic, new roads threaten our increasingly meagre natural resources and car culture strikes violently at our health and safety. Despite continued safety improvements, sheer weight of numbers keeps

the victims coming: over 18 million people have died at or under the wheels of the world's cars since 1885.

Serious attempts at turning the tide of automobility did not begin until it was too late, and the car had become socially, politically, economically and physically enmeshed into the fabric of the city. Despite this, the solution proposed by the car is now the problem. Although this reversal of emphasis superficially undoes modernist attempts to integrate highways with cities, car-centric planning shouldn't be dismissed out of hand. The blight caused by these schemes – the pedestrian decks, urban motorways, barren precincts and inhospitable car parks – only occurred because how and why we use our cars changed, numbers rose and congestion replaced freedom. Dependence has increased to the point where infrastructure is unable to cope.

Carchitecture dominates everyday life, and it is only in the last decade that popular opinion has started to question the wisdom of devoting time, energy, money and infrastructure to propagating car culture. In Europe at least, a seismic shift in public and political opinion has led to campaigns and legislation against automobile use, with some countries (notably Switzerland and Scandinavia) taking an advanced stand on unravelling the miasma that follows the car. However, the car's economic importance, not only as a commuting tool but as a source of export funds and tax revenue, has prevented other countries, especially in the Far East and the US, from prohibitive legislation. Large swathes of the planet are currently embarking on attempts to comprehensively integrate the car into their cities and economy, bolstered by economic assistance from beleaguered Western manufacturers. Cars, we are told, are costing us the earth. Yet they are also sustaining a substantial part of the economic system, however flawed, making a world without cars seem not only unthinkable but also financially catastrophic.

We continue to love our cars, unwilling to surrender their practicality and convenience. In an attempt to minimise congestion in the world's biggest conurbation, Mexico City (population 20 million), the authorities concocted a plan following extensive public consultation. In the late 1980s, permits were issued to all car owners which stipulated that on one day a week, to be determined by the number on their license plate, they were not authorised to drive. It was hoped that weekday car use would be reduced by 20%. Needless to say, the 'Today Don't Drive' scheme did not work out as planned. Despite initial support from car owners, many found that they were loath to take public transport one day a week. Within a year, the number of cars in the city had soared, as a significant number of people bought a second car, with a different license number enabling them to circumvent the ban. In December 1989, 2 million cars were on the streets at any one time. Within six years, that number had increased by 50%.

Clearly, legislation and official remonstration is not enough. Economic and social dependence confounds both best intentions and common sense. Commuting via car is habitually decried and denigrated: motorists are made selfish pariahs, choking children, crowding streets and contributing to the gradual decline of living standards. And yet magically, no one feels that these edicts are directed at him or her. The wasteful motorist, eschewing shoe leather for a 400 metre round-trip to a local shop, doesn't recognise their behaviour as aberrant or irresponsible, despite the fact that most people, to varying degrees, misuse their cars this way. And why should they feel

In August 1955, the one millionth Beetle rolled off the VW assembly line in Wolfsburg. Hitler's 'People's Car' had become a globally adored product, a genuinely mass-market object.

bad? Society – in towns, cities, villages everywhere – is structured around these short journeys, and all indications point to their increase, not decrease. School runs safeguard children, supermarkets offer value and convenience to the trolley-wielding, and therefore car-owning, shopper, public transport merely offers danger and delays. The anti-car lobby might reject these statements, yet for a great many people, in Europe, America and beyond, they represent the truth about their day-to-day lives.

The modernist obsession with mechanisation had its roots in the brave new world of mass production, the epic architecture of Detroit's cathedrals of industry and the unequalled sensation of speed conveyed by the new technology. Hopes were high. Not only would the automobile revolutionise the way people got around big cities, it would also bring about new ways of building houses – the machine for living in. Today, technology transference – the information and technology exchange between the car industry and architects – reveals not only deep-seated cultural differences between the two industries, but also the need to overcome contradictory political messages about the value of cars – and cities – within our society. The upper echelons of the housing market are dominated by products which stress the amount of craftsmanship and labour which have gone into their construction; mass-produced, mechanised building is the enemy of quality, taste and distinction. Yet no executive dream home can compare with even the most basic car, comprised of over 10,000 different parts.

For those who believe that working with rather than against the car is the best agenda, carchitecture's hybridity symbolises the fusion of two sets of technologies, perhaps going some way to resuscitating the discredited vision of the modernists. The car represents the model environment – hermetically sealed, highly efficient, swift to manufacture and easy to maintain. If only our homes and offices could learn from this compacted collection of technologies, a single unit incorporating all the comforts we have become accustomed to. Carchitecture therefore becomes a cause for optimism, signalling a new world of crossover, the sharing of technology and possible solutions to the dilemma of the car in the city. Many architects and designers acknowledge the influence of the mass-produced machine, not just through explicitly evoking the dynamic forms created for high speed travel, but in the use of secondary technologies developed for production, interiors and ergonomics.

Architectural solutions drawn from automotive technology reflect a desire to learn from the car, rather than submit meekly to its will. Yet the automobile's totemic power is hard to dispel. The car is still fetishised, in extreme cases it is literally placed on a pedestal within the home. Although cars are one of the most common objects on the planet, we are still drawn to the new, unusual and expensive. The automobile remains an indicator of wealth, of power and status, with our environment geared to its display, maintenance and use. The hyper-consumer environment of car dealerships, which line our arterial roads in multi-coloured strips from Essex to Palm Springs, lay bare this eternal fascination.

There seems to be no danger that automotive technology, with its emphasis on speed and efficiency, will be made redundant by the ever-increasing numbers of cars on the road. Regardless of the perils of total gridlock, manufacturers are diversifying into multi-purpose vehicles, ultra-small city cars, reconfigurable people carriers, sports utility vehicles, all giving us freedom from the road itself, not to mention new power

SERVICE STATION, M1

THE HAMMERSMITH FLYOVER, EASTBOUND

sources, clean fuels and a technological revolution that will transform our cars into mobile information centres. We are receptive, perhaps even too eager, for these new ways of navigating our world – the automobile is carefully designed to fulfil both our public and private aspirations.

In this sense, cars present us with a great dichotomy. One the one hand, they are the epitome of the perfect private environment, a hermetically-sealed pod that shelters us from the rigours of the outside world. On the other hand, we use our cars on the primary social spaces within the city – roads. This division is accentuated by the car's increasing role as home from home, offering ever more attractive, insular environments. Car advertising takes a similarly dualist approach: either the emphasis is placed on freedom and release, or on the promise of better integration into society – put simply, this car will help you make friends.

Visually, the car also forms a vital component of our world. As the most accessible 'design' object most people ever encounter, let alone own, new models help define our environment, shaping the way we see and perceive the future. Ford's Sierra (1982) was a pivotal moment in car design, a form initially pilloried as a jelly-mould yet subsequently adopted by every other manufacturer. More recently, with the Focus model, the company has again set a popular agenda, introducing a slashed angularity of remarkable modernity. In architecture, similar forms are found only in the work of determined avant-gardists whose spectacular projects remain defiantly isolated and unusual, defying convention.

Architectural history in its purest sense – the litany of styles, aesthetics and names – fails to address the lived experience of buildings. Architecture is a cultural object and as such it is not just the product of architects and town planners. Rather, it is a constantly evolving series of spaces, responding to and shaping social discourse, altering in turn to accommodate changes in cultural, commercial, personal and political issues.

Space – the city – is what we make of it. To divorce our experience of the city from the automobile is not only perverse, but also unrealistic. The history of the car in the city is not just about re-shaping the urban environment, but a myriad of other concerns. How regulations adapt to accommodate the dominant interest group – first the pedestrian, then the automobile, latterly the pedestrian again. How commuting distances create distinctions between our homes and offices, and increase our daily travel (now 45 km a day in Britain, up from 8 km a day in the 1950s) without broadening our horizons. Our experience of the car in the city is not qualified by the grand, overall utopias of modernism – despite their overwhelming pro-car stance. Even recent trends in town planning, which have taken the opposing position, rejecting auto-centric cities and advocating a return to walking, are not part of lived experience.

Instead, the car, like the pedestrian, forms a series of relationships with the city on an almost microscopic level, our eyes and senses growing accustomed to the signs, devices and movements that enable a safe journey. Slow for speed cameras. Watch for pedestrians. Be distracted by attractive passers-by. Accelerate between speed humps. Catch the lights. Find a parking space. Check the mirrors. Driving is a remarkably sensory experience. A journey across a crowded city, however slow, provides a plethora of experiences – architectural, social, physical, visual, spatial. The car has become a crucial device for decoding our perception of cities.

The automobile and architecture are not about to be separated. Predictions suggest

**BMW Junior Bike**
Born to be wild: to conquer the world on two wheels, but with extra quiet tyres if you please. Based on the full-size R 1100 GS.
Part no            Price
80 83 9 421 144   £65.00

**BMW Z3 Pedal Car**
No-compromise sporty styling, environmentally friendly and the centre of attention in every child's bedroom.
Part no            Price
80 93 9 430 502   £95.00

**BMW Baby Racer II**
The racer that drives kids wild: innovative technology matched with attractive design.
Part no            Price
80 93 0 006 909   £40.00

increased numbers. Sales are on the rise. Computer-generated images of the Bedfordshire Zero-Emission Development, BedZed, perhaps the most environmentally progressive housing ever built in Britain, featured a fleet of multi-coloured Smart cars, replacing hard-standings stacked with the Mondeos and Vectras of suburban tradition without banishing the car altogether. Even if car sizes are shrinking, official planning directives still require the majority of new housing developments to have a parking component.

The car has yet to be usurped. Despite vast financial incentives to design an alternative system, the car remains the epitome of personal transportation. Futurist transport visions focused on increased automation, speed, safety and efficiency, yet always centred around the independent, individual module. Despite the promise of technology to enable the highway and road to become a new space of social interaction, the pervasive belief that roads are by their very nature alienating and therefore impossible to integrate into the urban fabric remains.

Arguably, the main point overlooked in the ascendance of anti-car rhetoric is that the car is a social space. Cars have always been about display, a codified signifier of social, financial or even sexual status. Los Angeles lowriders, South London's car stereo wars, the Chelsea Cruise, custom culture the world over, even the autojumble or car boot sale; these are all intensely social pursuits, dependent not only on drivers but also on the presence of a non-driving audience.

Carchitecture means many things to many people; positive, negative, dismissive, oppressive. Yet to deny the car in the city is to deny our lived experience of urbanism. The automobile and architecture have always interacted, playing off one another in complex and inter-related ways. Today it is fashionable to decry the destructive intrusion of the car, claiming it has swept away traditional urbanism, leaving blockaded, decaying inner cities surrounded by sprawling suburbs. However, the future – the immediate future – will almost certainly be as focused on four wheels as the past 100 years. It is how those four wheels will look, and the ways in which we will use them, that will determine the carchitecture of tomorrow.

At a time when discussions about the role of cars in our society are central to political debate, lauding the structures, cross-pollination and influences that the internal combustion engine has had on our cities and landscape flies in the face of popular consensus: four wheels bad, two wheels (or, better still, two feet) good. But this is simplistic response to a complex problem. And as we have seen above, the ultimate goal – personal transport – generates contradictory approaches and emotional responses.

Perhaps there is a way forward. By acknowledging the social function of the automobile, we would not be taking another step towards catastrophe. For too long, carchitecture has come to symbolise the worst excesses – and consequences – of car-centric planning. Static cities, sprawl and environmental degradation are all consequences of unchallenging automotive devotion. Yet throughout all this time, the car has remained constant, whether pilloried or praised, shunned or embraced. As a consequence, we have become culturally indebted to automobiles, while deriding carchitecture as the bastard offspring of our obsession. Ultimately, in order to attain a transport system that reflects our true experience of the city, private and public will have to learn to co-exist. Carchitecture may be the past, but it is also the future.

**BMW Junior Racer**
For the heroes of tomorrow: the perfect combination of dynamism and comfort. Of course featuring the typical BMW look.
Part no          Price
80 93 0 022 078   £110.00

**BMW Z3 Battery-Driven Electric Car**
That's what a dream car looks like: from 0 to 6 km/h in 15 seconds, bright blue and, of course, "topless".
Part no          Price
80 93 9 430 503   £185.00

Prices include VAT

Pro-car propaganda starts young: 'Children love action, that's why BMW offers a wide range of products revolving around mobility. It goes without saying that all products have undergone ergonomic testing, are safe to use and are made to a tough and sturdy design. All to make sure that little BMW drivers also get their fun on wheels.'
(BMW Children's Range brochure)

# BRING YOUR OWN SPACE

HEATHER PUTTOCK

'Automobiles are like part-time dwellings on wheels'
Richard Buckminster Fuller.

If a car can be the symbol of an era, then the Multi Purpose Vehicle is the 1990s psyche objectified. From the 'People Carrier', such as the Renault Espace, to the 'compact' Nissan Tino and the 'van-based' Citroën Berlingo, with the Fiat Multipla niched somewhere in between, the MPV assimilates all the fixations of the pre-millennial age: safety, control, individuality, celebrity and leisure.

Of course the MPV is not actually a quintessentially 1990s concept. Its streamlined, aerodynamic form, and the 'omnimedium' thinking behind it, can be traced back to Norman Bel Geddes's teardrop-inspired vehicles of the late 1920s and Richard Buckminster Fuller's Dymaxion cars of the early 1930s.

But whilst modernity – speed, progress, glamour – screams from every pore of these early futuristic frames, the philosophy underpinning the contemporary MPV is manifestly less dynamic.

At the beginning of the last century, the motorcar introduced the idea of democratic mobility: once you were in a car you were a free person, you could go wherever you wanted to go and you were in control. A complexity of cultural and socio-economic concerns has now diminished that pioneering spirit – it is hard to be adventurous when the roads are gridlocked and the average speed is barely faster than

walking pace. From being enthralled by the motorcar we are now entrapped by it, and as a result, our attention, and that of the car designer, have turned inwards: if we are to spend longer and longer in our car, then it should duplicate our other static dwelling place, the home, as much as possible. MPVs have now become microcosmic 'living rooms' on wheels, often more perfect than the domestic

Left: The launch of the Espace in 1984 made Renault the first company to produce a mass-market MPV. Top: With the focus firmly on comfort and safety, the Avantime is Renault's top-of-the-range coupé for 2001. The designer, Thiery Metroz, cites the architecture of Le Corbusier and Richard Meier as influences on the car's angular lines. Above and opposite: The Fiat Multipla, which first appeared on our roads in 1999, is a multi-purpose six-seater in the spirit of the 1930s Topolino and the original Multipla from 1956. Less than four metres long, it comfortably seats six passengers in two rows of three.

spaces they seek to replicate. We may not be in control of the external environment, but by reinventing the car's interior space, the MPV has also re-empowered the disenfranchised driver, for here control is regained.

The sense of well-being that the MPV has induced has meant that a growing number of drivers now believe that MPV manufacturers are more concerned about safety than the makers of conventional vehicles. Erroneously, it would seem, as in a number of tests carried out by the New Car Assessment Programme (NCAP) the Multi Purpose Vehicle performed badly. Nevertheless, the MPV is increasingly seen as the practical choice for family motoring: 47,000 were sold in the UK in 2000, its usurpation of the Volvo's role as the middle class family car of choice having previously been underlined by Tony Blair's purchase of Chrysler Grand Voyager in 1997. The MPV had arrived.

Ironically, in a growing and increasingly crowded and competitive market the safety issue has been the bedrock upon which manufacturers have sought to base their move away from the original seven-seater people carrier to the creation of a compact MPV, which allows the driver to choose a

configuration of flexible seating or a large luggage capacity. In the preliminary stages of its research into the compact Tino, Nissan consulted the National Childbirth Trust to find out what parents want from a car. Front seats have been shaved and widened at the shoulder, whilst back seats are raised a few centimetres, all to maximise visibility. The centre chairs are fitted with an integral belt to ensure that young children are not put in (so the manufacturers tell us) often incorrectly installed car seats. A medical kit is also offered as an accessory. Moreover, a cornucopia of storage areas and the creative interior detail reflect Tino's aspiration to create what Buckminster Fuller referred to as the 'broken off part of the house': a covered tray and coin holder on

the dash board; open storage in the central console; a storage drawer under the front seat, two rear floor storage areas with jelly bean beach baskets; driver and front passenger door storage nets; small additional front door pockets; rear 1.5 litre bottle holders or rubbish tray; rear 12 volt socket; seat based tables with cupholders; pen holder on the back of the rear seat; nets in the boot area and cover for the rear luggage. But the wealth of interior design also highlights the manufacturers' desire to target the burgeoning sector of car-owning twenty-somethings, who wish to trade up their city runaround for a car that offers and accommodates a bigger and better lifestyle experience.

At the so-called Leviathan end of the market, the MPV has far loftier ambitions. The aeronautical symbolism of vehicle names like the Galaxy, Espace and Voyager hankers after a twenty-first century promise of space travel, but provides instead an American retro-rendering of an air flight and the VIP trip to the hotel afterwards. In the Voyager PT (for Personal Transport), there is plenty of leg room up at the front in first class; two business class seats in the mid-section have personal air conditioning while the rear bench acts as economy until, that is, you replace six of the seats with optional rotating, Captain-Kirk-style (if not quite up to La-Z-Boy standard), chairs. When the inflight entertainment has finished

– Ford now factory-fits videos or Playstation 2s as extras with monitors in the rear of the front headrests – the tinted glass cloaks the rear windows in a kind of celebrity reverie.

The ultimate goal of the MPV, however, is to remain car-like. Any suggestion of 'van-ness' is anathema to the MPV designer (except if the MPV in question is a Citroën Berlingo, which then emphasises its saloon-ness), particularly any associations with the VW Kombis of the 1960s, which could change functionality with the removal of the rear seats, and whose name became shorthand for a hippie woolly-mindedness. The new MPV and its descendants will be extremely serious and hi-tech about having fun. No concept cars like Mario Bellini's Kar-a-Sutra (1972), whose soft interior furnishings were intended for 'human and not automative rites'. Indeed, Nissan's new concept MPV, the three-door Chappo (the first MPV to be marketed as a 'living room on wheels'), is based on the expectation that in the future young people will use their cars as place to surf the net, watch DVDs and play computer games. The asymmetrical, tall, two-box car has an L-shaped seating plan which creates a large mobile social space in the middle. The steering wheel can be put flush with the dashboard at the touch of a button and the doors, which can be opened from either direction because each vertical edge has hinges and locks,

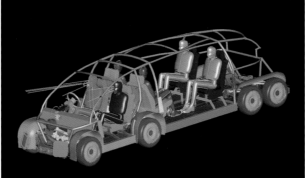

LIVING SPACE

WORKING SPACE

are also controlled electronically – just like a Dymaxion house. The Chappo also has two retractable screens: a seven-inch monitor that extends from the centre console and is 'user-information orientated' – providing GPS, air-conditioning and music-system control – and a fifteen-inch screen that offers DVDs, computer games and internet access through a keyboard located at the side of the vehicle.

The problem with the Chappo is that it is not a particularly charismatic car. It exudes neither style nor attitude, and it is hard to believe that it would appeal to its target audience. However, similar criticisms were levelled at the bug-eyed Fiat Multipla – heir to the 1956 model that was based on the Fiat 600 and functioned as a six-seater minibus – when it was launched, until people discovered that putting three seats at the front and moving the windscreen forward over the bonnet meant that six people and their luggage could be transported in comfort. Maybe as the boundaries of domestic and work space blur, the external appearance of the MPV will cease to matter, and the most important consideration will be the configuration of space, for as Fernand Léger argued in 1924, the more a machine perfects its utilitarian functions, the more beautiful it becomes.

Opposite above: With video monitors and internet access, the VW Microbus is far removed from the 9-seater camper van introduced in 1949. Opposite below: A collaboration between the Japanese Science and Technology Corporation and Italian design consultants IDEA, the KAZ (Keio Advanced Zero-emission) has eight electric motors, one for each of its eight wheels, allowing it to reach close to 300kmh.
Above: Nissan describe the Chappo concept city car, unveiled in 2001, as a 'living-room on wheels', a multi-functional space designed from the inside out.

# 2. THE FUELLING OF DESIRE

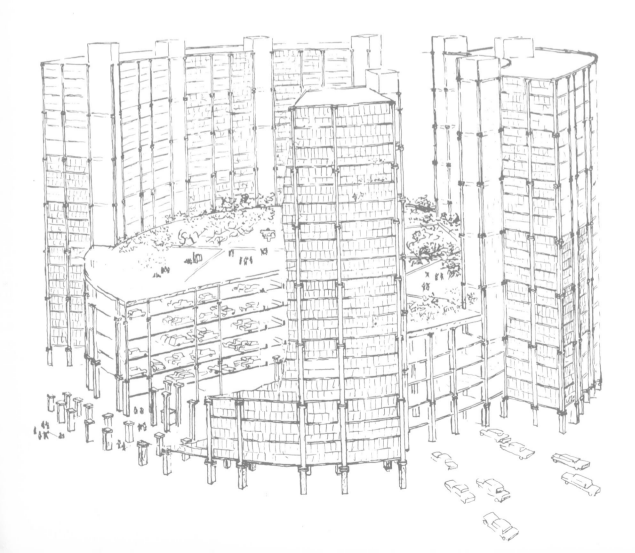

**'More than any other consumer good the motor car provided fantasies of status, freedom, and escape from the constraints of a highly disciplined urban, industrial order.'**

Clay McShane, *Down the Asphalt Path*, (1994)

The introduction of Ford's Model T in 1908 stripped away the hierarchical structure that had kept cars from the masses. By making the machine affordable, mass production revolutionised social interaction. Just under 6,000 Model Ts were sold in 1908 at $850 each, whereas eight years later over 370,000 were sold, each for less than $400. Between 1910 and 1930, Ford's home town of Detroit churned out some 5.3 million automobiles. At least half the city's workers were involved in the auto industry, and 'Autocity' faced a population explosion, growing from 300,000 at the turn of the century to 1.5 million in 1929. Although Detroit was the first city of its type, it provided a compelling model for urban success which was to be repeated throughout the world, in Turin, Wolfsburg, Dagenham, Mulhouse, Coventry and countless other cities. Transport had already heralded a change in the psycho-geography of the city, now mass production and mass consumption made the car a potent and dominant cultural symbol, a token of status and power that dazzled politicians, architects and the public.

As the automobile descended through the strata of class and wealth, mass motoring's enormous impact on the existing city was also translated into speculative visions of the city to come. Car-centric schemes, drawn up by starry-eyed architects, cut great swathes through the pre-motorised city, freeing the early motorist from the halting, filthy traffic of the pre-combustion era. Auto utopias are epitomised by the early work of Le Corbusier, whose unbuilt 1925 Plan Voisin for three million citizens took carchitecture to brave new heights, proposing to raze vast areas of Paris and replace them with a utopian environment that embodied his five points of architecture. 'The motor car has killed the great city; the motor must save the great city,' Le Corbusier wrote, full of optimism about a shiny, speed-filled future. The Plan Voisin was even named after the automotive firm that had sponsored his proposals; the car's futurist credentials were impeccable. Le Corbusier returned to the theme again and again. His monolithic 1932 Plan for Algiers advocated the location of housing beneath a vast, winding highway that curved along the Mediterranean coast. Corb's concept for Algiers was a development of a 1929 sketch for Rio de Janeiro, a sweeping highway elevated along office blocks: the road had become a dynamic component of the modern city. Yet it would be wrong to characterise Le Corbusier as a straightforward functionalist – he was passionately opposed to the development of the sprawling suburbs that he witnessed on visits to America after 1945. For Corb, the car was only useful to the city insofar as it could help bring about a better human and social environment, and even his most radical of city plans was founded on the extensive use of public, pedestrian space.

Autophilia was also inherent in art movements such as Russian Constructivism and Italian Futurism. Architect Konstantin Melnikov proposed a dramatic car park for Moscow in 1925, cantilevered high above the streets, the curves of the ramps forming the building's dynamic silhouette. The scheme was never built. His fellow architect

Opposite: American architect Louis Kahn's 1960s proposal for a car park merges building with road, using a simple concrete frame that functions as either office floor or parking. The garage roof also doubles up as an open space for office workers.

Mikhail Minkus designed a low-lying parking structure in 1931, also unbuilt, that exploited the modernist vocabulary of strip glazing and concrete vaults to create a grandiose 350-car garage. These schemes made explicit the connection between the dynamism conveyed by the automobile, the structural possibilities of new materials like concrete and the creation of an architecture which could soar and curve, expressing the joy of technology through solid form.

The Corbusian ideal became firmly lodged – and perhaps misinterpreted – in the minds of architects, planners and transport engineers, with dramatic consequences for the built environment. Geoffrey Jellicoe's *Motopia*, published in 1961, is Voisin-lite, the audacity (and verticality) of Corb's scheme filtered through Jellicoe's extensive landscaping experience and the British garden city vision of the previous century. *Motopia*, sponsored by Pilkington Glass, proposed a gridded city laid across the landscape, elevating buildings on pilotis amongst landscaped parklands, and placing all roads and access on the roofs above. Citing precedents like the Algiers Plan, Jellicoe's Motopia was a relatively low-density city of 30,000 persons, a brave attempt at creating a community that integrated cars, people and landscape. Like Le Corbusier, however, Jellicoe achieved this integration by keeping cars away from pedestrian areas, on a sweeping road system situated dramatically on the roofs of the buildings.

While Jellicoe tried to mitigate society's auto-centric determinism with a scheme which returned the city to pedestrians, others were less accommodating. Frank Lloyd Wright once described the city plan as a vortex, spiralling out from the needs of its occupants. In his 1932 essay, 'What Does the Machine Mean to Life in a Democracy', Wright explained how city planning should respond to the new age, rather than the 'man on his legs': 'But how to utilise [the city] plan now when the standard of space measurement has changed to a man seated in his motor car, vicarious power in the throttle at his feet, his hands on a steering wheel, not to mention the cigar in his mouth. One mile has little advantage to him over ten miles.' It was a sentiment that perceptively predicted the future suburban development of many American cities. Wright also passionately believed in the power of architecture to respond to the

Above and top: Written by G.A.Jellicoe in 1961, *Motopia: A Study in the Evolution of Urban Landscape* is a very English response to the Corbusian ideal, combining rolling landscape with polite brutalism.

Opposite: Artist Steven Brower's installation 'U-town' is a comment on American trailer-park culture, filtered through the Buckminster Fuller-influenced Drop City, Colorado, 1965. An alternative community, Drop City's geodesic domes were built from scrap cars.

emerging technology. 'You will be able to drive a motorcar up to the new house and not spoil the picture,' he said in 1932, unable to resist adding, 'You can't do that to the fashionable ones now if you are sensibly eye-minded.' Wright had designed a suburban house scheme with an integral garage as early as 1904.

Even classical, Beaux Arts planning was in love with the car. Architect Daniel Burnham, an autophile and visionary, spearheaded the City Beautiful movement, believing in arrow-straight boulevards – motorways before their time – for swift and unencumbered motoring, with great spokes of radial roads fanning out from monumental centres. More notoriously, 1930s Germany seized on the propaganda and political value of a fast, effective motorway system. The autobahn was explicitly integrated into the Nazi party aesthetic; sweeping bridges carried the four lane highways across valleys, while overscaled plazas, squares and colonnaded roadways formed a key part of Hitler's rebuilding plans for Berlin.

The car became the conduit for futurist expression. Norman Bel Geddes' 'Futurama' exhibit at the 1939 New York World's Fair was a prediction of the nation's road system in 1960. Bel Geddes, a pioneer of streamlining in its most commercial form, envisaged fourteen-lane highways and radio beams separating speeding cars to ensure safe distances were kept. The World's Fair descended on a post-depression America eager for vision. Its evocative corporate imagery promised a bolder, better America, and Futurama visitors were shown a world where highways, parkland, pedestrians and soaring towers coexisted in harmony. Bel Geddes' vision was rewarded by a role in President Roosevelt's National Motorway Planning Authority, the body that laid the groundwork for the country's interstates. The exhibit, also known as 'Highways and Horizons' and sponsored by General Motors, was prescient. 'I have seen the future', extolled the badge given to each visitor. It was the most popular exhibit at the fair.

Bel Geddes' intense vision deliberately confused his futuristic imagery with the contemporary products of the exhibit's sponsor. Like the US government, General Motors were also keen to make the connection between highways and prosperity. 'The "Futurama" is presented, not as a detailed forecast of what the highways of the future might be, but rather as a dramatic illustration of how, through continued progress in highway design and construction, the usefulness of the motor car may still be further expanded and the industry's contributions to prosperity and better living be increased,' read the exhibit's booklet. Futurama froze the values of the age in time, creating a mirror of contemporary theories, fears and aspirations. It also signified an escalation in the corporate control of imagination, allying technology – a commodity – with progress, both social and economic. GM had been here before, using their mighty 'Futurliner' concept vehicles at the Chicago Fair of 1933 to generate public interest in new models. Subsequent nationwide tours – 'Parades of Progress' – ensured that in the next twenty years nearly 12 million people saw the machines, great slab-sided bus-sized vehicles, cementing the connection between GM, progress and the American way; the car led the way to tomorrow. If Le Corbusier's *Modulor* aimed to formalise the importance of human scale in architecture, then the ascendance of the motor car added a completely different, time-based axis to the architectural equation: speed.

During this period of optimism, the passion for road building was uncontested. America's 42,000 miles of interstates were conceived by President Eisenhower, who had been inspired by the example of the German road network. Road building and

prosperity were synonymous; the architecture of cars was hailed as a generator and motivator for wealth and happiness. Today, the pro-roads movement continues to praise America's $300 billion investment in its Interstate system, hailing the Interstates as integral to the nation's economic and political superiority.

> 'Democratisation of mobility: The interstate highway system has facilitated an unprecedented expansion of mobility and in a democratic manner – no nation on earth can equal the mobility that is available to the overwhelming majority of Americans. More than 90% of the nation's households have access to automobiles.'
> *The Best Investment a Nation Ever Made*, Wendell Cox and Jean Love

The urge to spread out from city centres was of paramount importance to the early road builders. Cities were for leaving far, far behind, and the expressway, preferably elevated and accentuated with scenic dips, banks and curves that conveyed speed, progress and a panoramic vista of the destination, would provide the urban dweller with a vital escape route and also stimulate the growth of the suburbs. This rejection of urbanism predated the car. In Britain, Ebenezer Howard's *Garden Cities of Tomorrow*, published in October 1898, was massively influential, positioning itself at the vanguard of a new socially-conscious movement to re-house slum dwellers and clear the inner cities. New technologies – trains, trams, omnibus and electricity – were used to create de-centralised communities removed (in physical terms, at least) from the congestion, disease and poor morality of the inner city. Likewise, American developers sought to edge out of city centres, towards open, healthy space.

For these reasons, roads were welcomed. The optimism and enthusiasm that greeted Britain's motorway system – epitomised by Sir Owen William's audacious engineering during the 1950s (a collection of some 131 solid, artful bridges, with 'a shape that will always be remembered,' according to Williams) – reflected that the nation had been crying out for swift roads for nearly forty years. In 1924 a motorway scheme had been proposed to link London and Liverpool, but it only reached a Private Member's Bill before being dropped. When the Luton-Crick phase of the M1 was opened in 1959, it was a cause for national celebration; a symbol of confidence and technological achievement. Some hoped to go further. Joyfeed, a Birmingham-based arts collective devoted to cataloguing the flipside of the 'mediocre' urban experience, recall the euphoric, unfulfilled utopian experiment of their city's Bull Ring car park.

> 'The motorist/consumer was to leave their vehicle in a reception area, wherefrom it would be transported, by a machine, and slotted safely into the correct space with robotic precision. The process would be reversed at the end of the shopping trip, ensuring maximum efficiency and pleasure. But this was to prove a labour saving device too far, as the mechanism jammed, and the unfortunate test vehicle was abandoned, along with the dream. Some say that it remains there, frozen in time like an Egyptian king, entombed in the cavernous solitude of the proud, crumbling structure.'

The motorway also brought its own architecture; the petrol station, motel and service area, transitory spaces that developed into self-contained communities dependent solely on the road. Our cynical contemporary eyes have difficulties adjusting to this era of optimism. The photographer Martin Parr's lovingly compiled

Opposite: Buick's Roadmaster Skylark convertible debuted in 1953 as an anniversary special to celebrate 50 years of the company. The car was significantly different from the standard model, with a lowered windscreen line to give a sleeker look, as well as power steering, hood, windows, aerial and brakes. The 1954 model illustrated here was slightly less extravagant, yet still epitomises Detroit's stylistic obsessions: low waistline, fins and lashings of chrome.

Left: Introduced in 1949, Alec Issigonis's Morris Minor blossomed from a wartime prototype into the archetypal English automobile. The ash-framed Traveller debuted in 1954 and lovingly-maintained 'Woodies' still fly the flag for a nation forever half-timbered. Above and opposite:

Inside Design, Wilsonart International and architect Chris Dean collaborated on a special edition of the Airstream trailer, creating a new interior. The classic sleek aluminium outer shell, dating from 1935, was deemed impossible to improve.

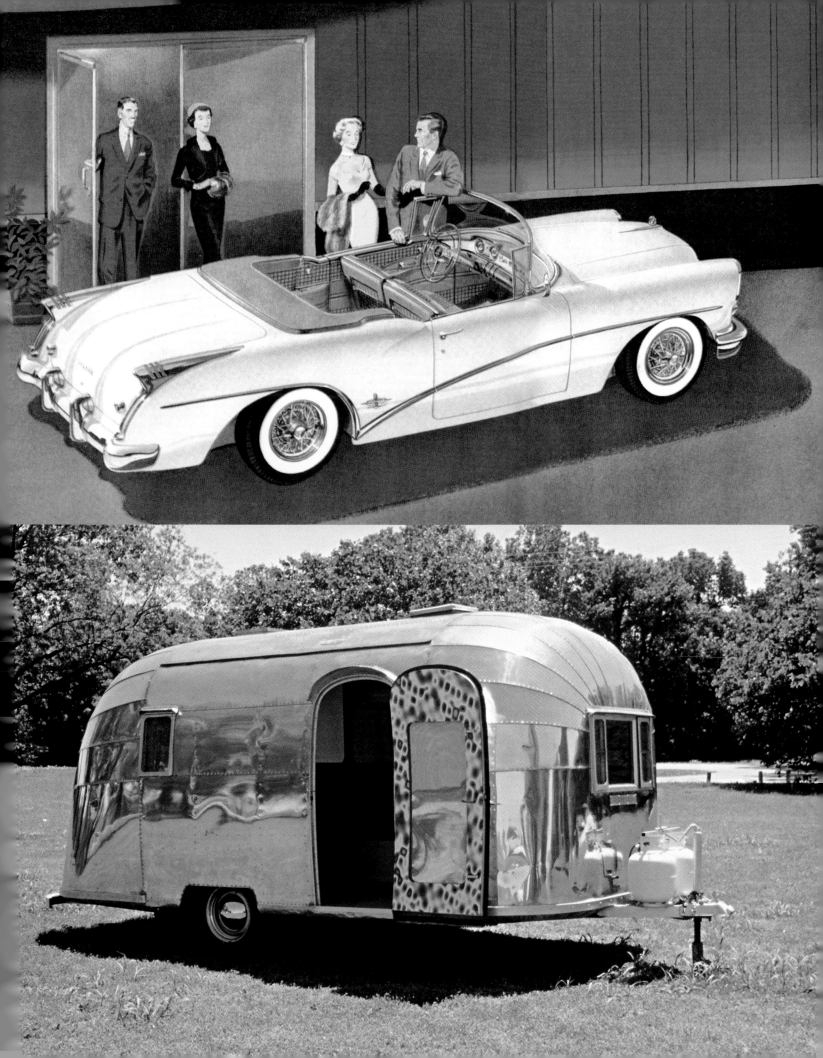

# THE AMERICAN DREAM

JONATHAN BELL

The post-war American experience of the automobile is perhaps the purest synthesis of national status and identity with a particular consumer product, a love affair largely unsullied by the harsh realities of environmental protest, high petrol prices and choked highways. Then, as now, automobile ownership was aspirational. Crucially, however, the 1950s saw the dawn of a new form of consumer car culture, an age of change when technology and culture was infused into the products of Detroit's production lines, creating unparalled states of desire.

According to historian Thomas Hine, the finned future was conjured up in a matter of moments by stylist Harley Earl, GM's skilled self-publicist who laid claim to the invention of the concept car and showed the auto giant the value – monetary, not scientific – of styling. Earl's snatched wartime glimpse of the then-secret Lockheed P-38 Lightning, with its twin tail-booms, first found its way onto the forecourt in the 1948 Cadillac. By the early 1950s, manufacturers who teased the tails of their models into slender fins were winning sales; conservative cars fell behind.

Thus began a great chapter in the automobile's history, an era of explicit comparison between the great technologies of the age – fighter planes, space travel and atomic power – and the consumer reality of the car. The rocket-style fins, jet exhaust details and dart-like trim were very visual symbols of speed and progress, with car advertising infused with aeronautical imagery. Concept cars came thick and fast, urging on next year's styling cues and feeding a hunger for novelty. Packard's 1956 show car was even called the Predictor, all the better to associate innovation with imminent consumer availability.

Automotive mobility fed and watered the icons of the American dream, the 3,000 square foot suburban detached house, containing a pliant spouse and 2.4 freckle-faced children, stacked full of labour-saving devices and a colour TV in the den. It was a lifestyle facilitated, if not entirely

created, by the two cars in the drive. This perfect picture of atomic family happiness was consummated through consumption, boosting America's economy, and making the rest of the world seem strangely bereft. 'Many things you've shown us are interesting but they are not needed in life,' mused a puzzled Nikita Kruschev during his famous 'kitchen debate' with Richard Nixon on 24 July 1959, 'They have no useful purpose. They are merely gadgets.'

Merely gadgets was exactly what the consumer desired. No other consumer object led a better campaign against communism than the automobile. The invention of air conditioning, electric windows, push-button transmission and radios were touted, year on year, as great leaps in comfort, convenience and class. In the same way that streamlining was far more effective as a 'metaphor for progress' in the pre-war auto industry, not as a

scientifically sound method for improving car performance, the styling cues of Detroit baroque also symbolised the future without necessarily providing any technical advantages. It hardly mattered; car styling was raw symbolism for a nation reared on the image.

Le Corbusier's fascination and horror with the chromium-plated jaws of these peculiarly American monsters wasn't shared by the general population. As the sleekly styled rocket-shaped saloons gradually overtook the bulbous cars and ersatz 'woodies' of the pre-war era, the very model names of these new machines signalled the dreams of the age; Meteor, Hornet, Wasp, Super Wasp, Century, Roadmaster, Customline, Firedome, LeSabre, Thunderbird, Galaxie, Comet and Star Chief, offered in Super, Special, DeLuxe, Super Deluxe and Special Deluxe models. The features that they sported, too, promised technology beyond most people's wildest dreams; Hydra-matic drive, Thriftmaster, Fluid Drive, Ultramatic, Dynaflow, Loadflight push button transmission and Overdrive. A push-button future was promised, and now it was being delivered.

Car-buying increased dramatically. In 1955, national spending on automobiles was $65bn, GM produced its one millionth car and became the first company to earn a billion dollars in a year. Automobiles were economically and culturally integrated – the only way these levels of spending could be sustained was to encourage frequent model changes, urging the consumer to follow fads and upgrade their ride as often as possible.

Commercial architecture adapted to accommodate this optimism, with the swooping concrete curves of Googie, a candy-coating for the new age. But the sudden increase in car ownership was also indicative of the flight to the suburbs. Googie was modernism dipped in Hollywood, the exaggeration of structural audacity for the purposes of aesthetic display. Not for nothing are the best examples of the style closely connected to the road – drive thrus, cafes, garages, drive-ins, bowling alleys – their signs acting as typographic totem poles to signal their presence from the road. Cultural historians cite the mass of imagery that indexed idealised suburbs, the picket-fence paradises of *I Love Lucy* and *Leave it to Beaver*, as well as official propaganda that promised safety, space, comfort,

convenience and community out of city centres. Home owning was also pitched as a defence against godless, property-bereft communism, ever present in the popular imagination.

In addition, suburbs benefited from the so-called 'white flight' (white collar, as well as skin), as families moved away from urban areas following the 1954 ruling to desegregate public schools. Levittown, the identikit suburb that bloomed in 1947 on the flat Long Island landscape, became the blueprint for a bindweed-like suburban pattern that swiftly engulfed the landscape. Early covenants on the land specifically forbade blacks from buying into the Levittown ideal, the sinister flipside of these allegedly perfect houses, standing on immaculate lawns.

Car names also reflected this brave new environment – the Chevrolet Nomad and Suburban, the Chrysler Town & Country. A nation weaned on the promise of a better future could find a space in its driveway for the Ford Galaxie Country Squire, a wood-panelled, V8-powered, nine-seater that took the nuclear family on a road trip to Yellowstone in perfect comfort, courtesy of the Cruise-O-Matic transmission. Along the way, gas

stations would offer full services – with pumps manned by attendants who'd also wash your windshield and check your oil levels.

The suburbs owed their existence to cars, which in turn became powerful symbols of America's social and economic status, signifying national strength through consumption. Arguably, cars played a key role in the Cold War, a crucial cog in the military-industrial machine. After all, the be-finned, winged creations that were emerging from Detroit were just a few steps along the scale from the new breed of jet fighters that had triumphed against the communist threat in Korea and were now promising safe and friendly skies against any Soviet invasion. Keeping a Cadillac in your driveway was subconscious support for rampant militarism – after all, the damn Russkies had to make do with lumpen, tinny Volgas.

As the 1950s faded out, a new cynicism entered the consumer consciousness. Advocates of industrial responsibility, most notably Vance Packard (*The Waste Makers*, 1960) and Ralph Nader (with *Unsafe at Any Speed*, 1965), started to question the system. Nader's 1965 book was a damning

report into the abilities of the Chevrolet Corvair, a car so unstable it was hazardous to simply turn the wheel. No lessons were learned from this in the perilous Ford Pinto, whose poorly placed fuel tank led to several fatal post-accident fires, and today we have the Ford Explorer, with its disastrous use of Firestone tyres, and the failure of the Mercedes A Class to pass the infamous Scandinavian 'Moose Test'.

It's easy to carp at this period of rampant enthusiasm, and highlight the failures of the political and social underpinnings of the age. The American dream was expressed through a collective national autophilia, setting the stage for a half a century of slavish adherence to the diktats of the car.

'Impressions? Yes. Impressions of a never-ending road.... Thrills? Yes. Thrills of scenery that would be worth stopping for if only there were time.... Trophies? Yes. Trophies to bring back memories of this day of travel: postcards, toy balloons and paper bathing girls.... Surely it is worth no man's while to drive three hundred miles from break of dawn on Sunday just to add another pennant to his string'.
Charles Merz, *The Great American Bandwagon*, 1928

Opposite: Avowed showman Harley Earl's 1950 concept car set General Motors's aesthetic agenda for a decade; practically every styling feature from the LeSabre would make it to the production line.
Opposite above: Chrysler's stylistic vocabulary distilled into pure form.
Above: The future made visible. General Motors claimed that the Firebird II (1956) was 'tailoring car design to gas turbine power.' Designed for the 'Highway of the Future,' the concept was advertised as the perfect car for the everyday family of four.
Left: Long, low and sleek – the contemporary home was a perfect match for the autos of the era.

*Boring Postcards* trilogy neatly summates the post-war predilection – and celebration – of carchitecture. *Boring Postcards* is a knowingly dishonest title – these images are anything but. Page after page of unsneering takes on the nascent bypass aesthetic reflects the feelings of the age; the architecture of roads and highways was a brave new world, the technicolor optimism bleeding from the page.

Commerce, and the architecture of commerce, underwent an evolutionary change. The rise of the drive-in and drive-thru – be they cinemas, fast-food stalls, banks, drug stores or chapels – have all capitalised on the freedoms afforded by four wheels. The drive-in movie theatre is the ultimate architectural colonisation of space, a fan-shaped asphalt spread that delivered entertainment, food and several levels of social interaction, all from the comfort of your car seat. By 1958 there were 5,200 drive-ins in America, making an entirely car-centric lifestyle possible:

> 'The drive-ins of the 1950s offered speedometer bingo, driving ranges, fishing ponds, open-air dance floors, miniature golf, toy trains that ran around the base of the screen beauty parlours, Laundromats. Many even celebrated church services on Sunday.'
> 'Spirit in the Sky', Richard von Busack, *San Francisco Metro*, June 1996

Roads were not only escape routes – they could also bring one into the city, spurring regeneration and dynamism. The advent of the car allowed for the exponential growth of cities, and also gave access to a workforce that lived far outside their physical boundaries: carchitecture added the dormitory town to its growing inventory of urban typologies. The great age of road-building in Britain, the 1960s, was combined with an emphasis on urban renewal and an almost manic desire to re-shape the creaky, bomb-damaged inner city in the image of America. The separation of pedestrians and cars was planning's holy grail. Peter Hall's *London 2000* (1963), an extended thesis on London's need for three orbital motorways, proposed cutting through large swathes of crumbling and unloved Georgian building stock, creating entirely new inner city districts specifically designed to accommodate a mobile, car-owning population. Hall created a London family of the future – the Dumills – who would live some 61 miles from Charing Cross at a proposed new town called Hamstreet in Kent. Although public transport exists, the Dumills' lives and environment is shaped and defined by the car. Leaving the house for the daily commute, 'their paths will never cross on the same level; the road system of Hamstreet, planned in a series of gigantic one-way loops, passes under and over the

Above and opposite above: When Mario Bellini conceived the 'Kar-a-sutra' in 1974, he saw it as a 'proposal for a micro-environment'. He collaborated with Citroën and Pirelli to make the prototype, before becoming a design consultant for Renault in the late 1970s. The Renault Espace was launched after he left, fuelling a belief that he was never fully credited for creating the original MPV.
Left and opposite below: Newell motor coaches are the Rolls Royce of the American RV (recreational vehicle) scene, custom-built to the owner's specification, no expense spared. Interiors are wildly fantastical – cantilevers allow the master bedroom to expand out of the main body of the coach. This is the vehicle as building: 'Wherever you are, from the rocky shores of Maine to the sunny sands of the California coast and all the miles between them, we want this to be an accommodation that you, your family and your guests can come home to with pride.'

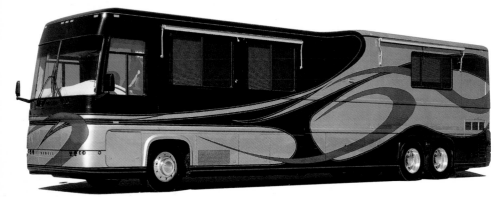

### Car rallies

Every weekend, all over Europe, ordinary people get into their cars and drive long distances to look at a bunch of other cars of exactly the same make and model as their own. Journey down any British motorway on a Sunday morning, and you are likely to overtake a convoy of VW Beetles, Minis, MGs or Triumphs, all heading for a rural field in which they will carefully be arranged in a proud, gleaming line. These are intensely social occasions, with the cars' owners likely to know one another from previous meetings: if you are an outsider you will certainly feel that mysterious knowledge has already been imparted to the knowing few. But what do the beaming owners actually find to discuss with one another? Their cars, of course. On countless fields across the land, information is being exchanged about chrome, steel, rubber, vinyl and paint. Serial numbers are memorised, measurements compared, ideas traded in the form of cubic centimetres, kilometres and amperes. Tiny differences between vehicles are celebrated: the Dormobile interior is compared with the Westfalia, and this in turn with the Viking, the Caravelle, Danbury, Devon or Moonraker. Here, the goal is to be just a little bit different: or at least that's the impression they want to give. In fact, by creating a 'unique' car where the difference lies in the colour of the interior carpet, or the shape of the rear light cluster, these owners serve only to emphasise how deeply ingrained are the details of mass-produced cars on the popular imagination. Every marque has its own owners club, sometimes clubs exist just for individual models. Mass-produced cars breed sprawling, populist memberships, while hand-crafted models retain an aloof and elitist crowd.

pedestrian alleys and paths, and finally converges on a main spine road under the quarter-square-miles of pedestrian deck which carries the town centre.' Hall's pro-motorway stance – since softened – was typical of the era, envisaging an age of utopian, auto-centric urbanity, the logical conclusion of contemporary thinking.

'... as the Dumills drive out of London by the New Kent Motorway, the expressways of London are a brilliant sight. When the first ones were built, back in the late sixties, the pessimists confidently predicted that they would wreck London. By 2000 most people admit that they gave it a new dimension, now trenching by the side of railways, now flying over rooftops, now burrowing through the heart of reconstructed shopping and office centres.'

The message was simple; the city and the motorway – autobahn, expressway, freeway, highway, dual carriageway, autoroute, autostrada – could co-exist. These great roads are the automobile's most explicit form of imposition on the environment. A linear building, made up of thousands of individual components – our cars – the motorway is carchitecture personified. Road building could overcome any problem; back in the late 1950s, engineers seriously proposed using helicopters to remove stalled cars from LA's broad, clogged freeways – anything to maintain the flow. American Highways, like German autobahns, were partly driven by military expediency; Eisenhower realised their potential as rapid evacuation routes in the face of the ever-imminent enemy invasion. The 1956 Federal Aid Highway Act put the American road-building programme in high gear by providing joint federal and state funding for highway building. Cold War culture was car culture.

The Interstate System was overseen by Frank Turner, the Federal Highway Administrator. Adjusted for size and population, America's highway system is now the densest in the world, 6.5 times the size of Britain's, and nearly 10 times the size of Japan's. The population welcomed it unquestioningly; even the advance of sprawl was spun as increased choice, not urban blight. By 1952, 85% of American travellers went by car, and two thirds of these stayed in the new roadside motels that sprang up alongside junctions and on the edge of towns. This was a world in which it seemed that technology could never fail society. One hundred years after the Industrial Revolution, progress continued to be made; horizons continued to expand, and the possibilities never ceased. Automotive technology, which was developing comfortably in parallel with military and aerospace research, offered the possibility for holidays and leisure, as well as for better machines in the home. The by-products of car culture were everywhere to be seen: by-passes and flyovers; lay-bys and slip-roads; car parks and car-ports; showrooms and breakers' yards; traffic lights and the highway code; roundabouts and T-junctions; road movies and garage bands; breakdowns, car crashes and inevitably, traffic jams.

A broad road and plenty of traffic equated progress. The development of Brasília, masterplanned by Lúcio Costa and Oscar Niemeyer and inaugurated in 1960, is one of the grandest evocations of modernist thinking. Brazil's new, dedicated, capital, was distinctly zoned, with government buildings and administration in the centre and residential wings spreading on either side. Each wing was sub-divided into neighbourhoods, or *superquadras*, arranged around local amenities and separated by a road system that kept pedestrians and fast traffic apart. The city could, both

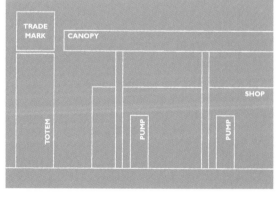

Below: Spanish designer Martí Guixé's explanatory drawing for Autoband, an adhesive tape complete with highway markings, designed as an ironic child's toy. Intended to raise abstract concepts of space, property and politics, the tape is intentionally hard to remove.

metaphorically and literally, spread its wings yet still accommodate pedestrian scale.

Carchitecture is elastic, stretching the parameters of our cognisance in order to hold our attention. And in turn, it has succeeded in drawing us into our cities, focusing economic activity at the urban centres, and changing the status of the city to the point where it is now more important than the nation state. Ever-bigger signs; longer, lower buildings; off-ramps that barely curve as they link colliding freeways; retail parks and service centres that expand exponentially the closer they are to a road: these are the products of the era of carchitecture. As speeds increased, our world has stretched; ramps lengthen, curves become shallower, architecture longer, lower and leaner.

Is the automobile's current position of dominance a consequence of modernist determinism? Or was the modernist response actually the best available strategy for accommodating the sudden surge in car ownership? Either way, utopia and autopia became enmeshed, a unity perpetuated by the willing collusion of governments, manufacturers, planners and the public. No problem was insurmountable: asphalt was the solution. Future visions were merely enhanced contemporary scenarios, assisted by technology to ever greater efficiencies. From metalled roads to off-ramps, workshops to assembly lines, motorways to car parks, service stations to motels, the car has shaped the architecture of the past century like no other object.

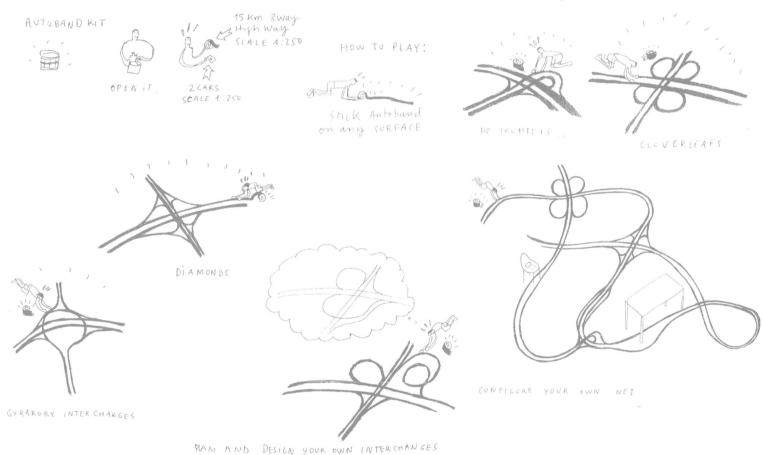

## Roundabout

In the late 1970s, it would have been possible to leave Britain for three years and believe upon returning that the country had suffered some kind of invasion. This was the period when the roundabout revolution took place, and hundreds of traffic intersections were replaced by circular islands. Everywhere, grassy mounds were constructed, and traffic suddenly found it possible to wind its way round

with much less congestion than during the reign of the traditional junction. The planners of the new town of Milton Keynes found roundabouts so irresistible that they based an entire city grid on them. It wasn't a purely British phenomenon, either: even the French eventually learnt to love the *Rond Point*, discovering its potential as a new location for displays of civic pride through brightly-coloured bedding plants (although the Gallic navigation system

was inevitably different from the British version). But sadly, the love affair with this miracle of traffic flow was to be diluted. In an increasingly commercial culture, the roundabout became one of the first public spaces to become dominated by sponsorship. In Milton Keynes, each and every roundabout is dedicated to a commercial angel – a reminder that this city is thriving thanks to that awesome combination of the Free Market and the Freeway.

Elsewhere, the plague is less widespread, but it is increasingly likely that the green central island on your nearest roundabout will be badged with a plaque commemorating the generosity of Hudsons Plumbers' Merchants, the local Building Society or a slightly dubious private organisation.

## Slip roads

Filtering into fast-flowing motorway traffic from a slip road is a matter of nerve and timing: this is one occasion when taking it slowly doesn't necessarily make things safer. Slip roads are about anticipation and transition, their purpose encapsulated in the moment when we can put our foot down, speeding up to match the traffic we're about to join. They serve to lead us into and out of a heightened state: on leaving the motorway, we can ease off, relax and re-adjust to the slower pace and the different view. Once, slip roads were the natural habitat of hitchhikers, who could be spotted hanging around the off-ramps of Europe, caught in limbo on their way somewhere – anywhere – else. Now, hitchhikers are an endangered species, another casualty of our ever-increasing levels of car ownership and our fears for personal safety. Being somehow neither one thing nor the other, solely a linking device, slip roads seem to lend themselves to acts of transgression, to liminal moments and wayward behaviour. They are the scene of desperate drivers' misguided attempts at damage-limitation, those occasions when reversing up or down a slip road to make up for a wrong turning suddenly seems like a good idea – much better than continuing until the next junction, at any rate. While these and similar lapses in judgement do little for road safety standards, they make for grimly fascinating TV viewing, providing ample material for cheap documentaries about 'drivers from hell': transgressive behaviour captured on CCTV in the name of entertainment.

Decq and Cornette's Motorway Operations Centre at Nanterre, France, exhibits a dynamism utterly compatible with its function. The angular building clings to the underside of the autoroute, simultaneously stealthy and overtly expressive of the cars rushing by just metres above.

Overleaf: Manuelle Gautrand's motorway toll booths and rest areas on the A16 in France playfully disregard bland roadside environments. In particular, the screen-printed canopies at Picardy bring to mind the stained glass of nearby Gothic cathedrals.

Opposite: Steinmann & Schmid's Parkhaus Saas-Fee (1997) acts as both a monument to anti-car culture and the aesthetic the automobile helped to engender. The 11-storey concrete and glass structure stands outside the ski resort of Saas-Fee in the Swiss Alps. Like many Swiss resorts, Saas-Fee is car-free, meaning that visitors have to deposit their vehicles at the Parkhaus for the duration of their stay.

The building's unashamed brutalism – all poured concrete and rigid modernist lines – stands against an alpine backdrop without concession to a rural aesthetic.

Above: This fire station in Maastricht, The Netherlands, designed by Neutelings Riedijk and completed in 1998, takes the aesthetic of the building's large roller doors and applies it to the whole façade.

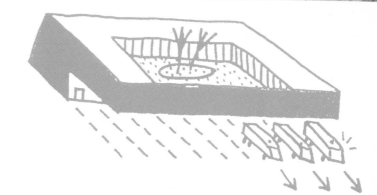

Neutelings Riedijk's Road and Water Support Building in the Dutch town of Harlingen is a work station for the maintenance and inspection of local roads. Designed entirely around practical considerations, 90% of the floor area is at the same level to allow vehicular access. Clad in black concrete panelling, with broad road-markings at ground level, the building deliberately evokes the utilitarian function of the road sign.

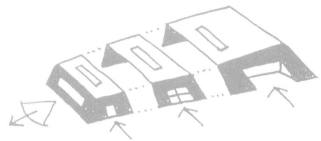

# CITROËN DS

NICK
BARLEY

Perhaps it was Roland Barthes' famous essay; or it may have been the enduring image of Charles de Gaulle riding in triumphalist multi-car processions through Paris in the early 1960s. Whatever the cause, the Citroën DS became – and has always remained – a firm favourite among architects and designers, an icon of experimental thinking in the face of ubiquitous automotive banality. Yet in spite of this passion, for twenty-five years after the last one rolled off the production line, Citroën did its best to distance itself from the DS. Some of Citroën's senior executives even wanted all remaining examples removed from Europe's roads. The marque's reputation for innovation rapidly waned, and throughout the 1980s and 1990s the company which had once launched the most radical car design of the 20th century became renowned for cars of dreary mediocrity.

What prompted this corporate change of heart? It is difficult to understand why a company should wish to turn its back on a car which has received such sustained adulation for nearly half a century. First, there was the explosion of publicity to accompany the car's launch: a fraught relationship between the secretive Citroën and the *Auto Journal*, whose scoops kept the French public on pre-launch red alert, and then such massive launch press coverage that in France it was beaten only by the death of Stalin for column inches. Next there was the triumphant unveiling, with 12,000 cars sold on the opening day of the Paris Car Show in 1955, and a string of canny publicity stunts to satiate buyers while early production difficulties were resolved. Most importantly, the *Déesse* itself rewrote the rules of automobile design. The list of innovations was breathtaking: frameless windows and a translucent fibre glass roof (both to maximise the light inside the car); an enormous aluminium bonnet at the front (the largest single piece of aluminium ever used in a car), and almost no overhang at the rear; a single-spoke steering wheel and space-age dashboard. But all of these paled into insignificance beside the greatest innovation of all: the hydraulic suspension. This was a car which floated on gas and liquid, a car whose steering, brakes and gear change were powered by hydraulic fluid. One touch of the mushroom-shaped brake pedal, and the car would oblige with a brutal emergency stop. A gentle nudge of

KOMFORT WIE NOCH NIE

Mit 2,25 qm

Scheibenfläche,

sind Sie

der europäische

Fahrer

der am besten

sieht.

the tiny dashboard mounted gear-lever (a clutch? how old fashioned!), and the car would smoothly shift up a gear. Many of the innovations were so far ahead of their time that they still seem radical today, and the chutzpah of the launch extended to the car's marketing material. In contrast to the hollow machismo of Harley Earl's American designs of the time, the DS offered formal elegance, functional sophistication, and technical tricks as radical as the atomic bomb. Here was a car to make an entire nation stand proud again. Here, in short, was the epitome of modernist design.

Needless to say, the extreme complexity of this exquisite machine resulted in problems, with high-profile celebrities angrily stricken by the roadside, having to call out the mechanics to get their sunken vehicle mobile again. Worse, Citroën faced deep embarrassment when it emerged that the red hydraulic fluid – the

DS's lifeblood – was highly corrosive to the metal pipes that transported it through the system. Most of the early cars literally ate themselves.

The cost of changing to a new fluid was one of several financial blows that the company was to incur during the 20-year life of the vehicle. And although the DS was special enough to win third place in a recent vote for the Car of the Century, its total lifetime sales of just 1.5 million compare with 15 million for the Model T Ford, and 5 million for the Mini. In the end, the DS cost Citroën a fortune, leading to its eventual sale to arch rival Peugeot, and giving the marque a reputation for unreliability that it grew desperate to shake off. But architects have reserved a special affection for the DS, and its legacy will remain long after the financial details have been forgotten. For many designers it remains the most innovative car of all time.

'The *Déesse* is obviously an exaltation of glass, and pressed metal is only a support for it. Here, the glass surfaces are not windows, openings pierced in a dark shell; they are vast walls of air and space, with the curvature, the spread and the brilliance of soap bubbles...

We are therefore dealing here with a humanized art, and it is possible that the *Déesse* marks a change in the mythology of cars. Until now, the ultimate in cars belonged rather to the bestiary of power; here it becomes at once more spiritual and more object-like, and despite some concessions to neomania (such as the empty steering wheel), it is now more homely, more attuned to this sublimation of the utensil which one also finds in the design of contemporary household equipment.'
Roland Barthes, *Mythologies,* (1957)

So steht der DS 19 nun vor Ihnen : klar in seiner Form, ein harmonisch geschlossenes Ganzes, das den Anforderungen des Verwöhntesten modernen Fahrers gewachsen ist, und zugleich unaufdringlich, doch deutlich in die Zukunft weist.
Und bedenken Sie bitte dabei, dass die diesem Wagen eigene Harmonie der Formen, die Sie zunächst als Schönheit empfinden, eigentlich nichts anderes ist als das plastische Endergebnis langjähriger Forschung und vielfachen Prüfens. Dieser Arbeit widmete sich ein Stab von Citroën- Ingenieuren und -Technikern, die in erster Linie einen zuverlässigen, soliden Gebrauchsgegenstand schaffen wollten, und deren Denken nur auf Zweckmässigkeit und Bewährung, auf Strassenlage, Leistung, Stromlinienforschung, Komfort und Sicherheit gerichtet war.

DIE LUST DER AUGEN

Denn wo das Strenge mit dem Zarten,
Wo Starkes sich und Mildes paarten,
Da gibt es einen guten Klang.

SCHILLER

Erst in den genau abgesteckten Grenzen, die ihm die strengen Masstäbe des Technikers vorschrieben, durfte der Modellist seine schöpferische Phantasie entfalten. So kam der Entwurf dieser einzigartigen Karosserie zustande. Da wurde beste Tradition aufgenommen und neu gestaltet, da wurde auch jede billige Zutat als störend oder kitschig verworfen, und nur das Eine Wesentliche im Auge behalten : die schlichte, lautere Schönheit.
Einmaliger Einklang von erlesenem Geschmack und Sachlichkeit, von Anmut und Zweckmässigkeit liegen der « funktionellen Schönheit » dieses Wagens zu Grunde. Auf zahlreichen Ausstellungen im Inland war den Schöpfern des DS 19 Citroën ihr Erfolg bereits bestätigt worden : doch der Weltruf dieser Karosserie wurde im Jahre 1957 begründet, als sie die Jury der berühmten internationalen Ausstellung für angewandte Kunst, der MAILANDER TRIENNALE, mit der bisher noch nie verliehenen höchsten Auszeichnung bedachte.

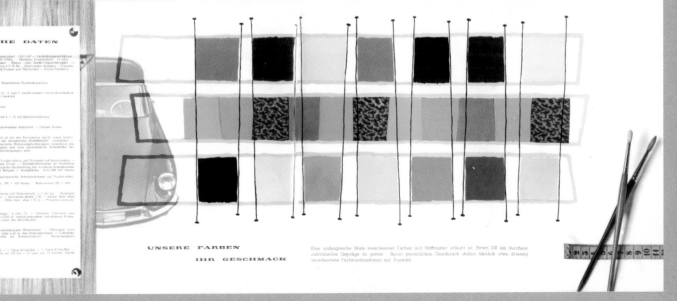

TECHNISCHE DATEN

MOTOR

KUPPLUNG

GETRIEBE

ZAHNSTANGENLENKUNG

ANTRIEB

FAHRGESTELL

AUFHANGUNG

BREMSEN

GEWICHT – ABMESSUNGEN

FASSUNGSVERMÖGEN

KOMFORT

FAHRWERTE

UNSERE FARBEN
IHR GESCHMACK

Eine umfangreiche Skala auserlesener Farben und Stoffmuster erlaubt es, Ihrem DS ein durchaus individuelles Gepräge zu geben. Ihrem persönlichen Geschmack stehen nämlich etwa dreissig verschiedene Farbkombinationen zur Auswahl.

# AGAINST AUTOMOBILE AUTISM

## ALEX STETTER

Some people consider cars to be inherently selfish objects, isolating drivers from their fellow urbanites in hermetically-sealed metal pods, but the automobile is an integral element of the contemporary city. Design groups bibi∗gutjahr in Germany and N2 Design in Switzerland organised the 'drive in' project to help bring out the car's sociable side. Max Borka, the Director of the Interieur Foundation and Interieur Design Academy I/De/A in Kotrijk, Belgium, sums up the spirit of the project: 'It appears that manufacturers' obsession with sales figures has caused them to overlook something very important: There is an element of autism in the automobile as it currently populates our world – though it shows flashes of technological genius, it is a social misfit.' N2 and bibi∗gutjahr brought together an international group of designers to reconsider the role of the car in today's world, and find new ways of reintegrating it into society. The results range from a pedestrian-friendly vehicle with soft, padded edges by Radi Designers in Paris, which was inspired by their observation that the airbag is a useful but egotistical invention, to Berlin-based designer Werner Aisslinger's scheme to recoup the high costs of running a car by turning into an illuminated, three-dimensional advertising billboard when parked at night. All the proposals were shown at the 2001 International Furniture Fair in Cologne.

Above: Beirut-based Karen Chekerdjian would like parked cars to function as personalised urban street furniture, with a fold-down public bench at the back and an aerial that doubles up as a bird table. Right: Spanish designer Martí Guixé suggests growing aromatic plants in the car to act as an organic air freshener. Drivers will also start to appreciate rain as a useful opportunity to water their flowers.

Right: 'drive in' logo by bibi*gutjahr, Cologne. Far right and below right: Our cars may have become homes on wheels, but London-based design team El Ultimo Grito, working with Ilka Schaumberg and Raki Martinez, bring the car right into the home. Below: Cities have been reaching for the sky for years, so why shouldn't cars follow suit? The SKYCAB, by Konstantin Grcic with Juliane Witte, Munich, turns the stretch limousine on its side, with standing room only for six.

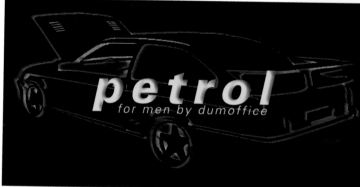

Left: A new concept in aftershave by Dumoffice in Amsterdam brings a whole new dimension to the distinctive aroma of the petrol station forecourt: 'The car. The man. The fragrance. A brilliant meeting of energy and masculinity. He loves action and thrives on challenges, allowing himself to explore options and adventures boldly.'

THIS
MACHINE

IS NOT
WORKING

# STYLE, RETRO AND TECHNOLOGY

Has the car responded to architecture? The car shaped the modern architectural vision, yet was this a two-way relationship? Perhaps the most persuasive collision between the built and mechanical environment was the golden age of streamlining in the 1930s. Architecture's brief dalliance with slippery forms owed a debt to the relentless promotion of the style in the 1930s, notably by major car firms like General Motors. Yet aside from this brief period of synergy, the mass-produced automobile has remained stylistically and aesthetically detached from the surroundings it travels through.

Today, the design diversification encouraged by shared platforms, market segmentation, strategic alliances and an increasingly visually literate consumer have placed the design of our cars on the top of agenda. Architecture, too, is beginning to draw influence and inspiration from the automobile, bringing about changes to the landscape that are nothing short of revolutionary. CAD and car-building techniques have opened up new possibilities for architectural design, and the impact of the car on architectural and urban thinking is entering a new era.

Cars might appear to be the natural enemy of architecture, yet architects disagree. If there's one object unduly fetished by the profession, it's the car. As we have seen, modernism and the automobile are synonymous, with great swathes of innovative architecture in thrall to its power. Physically, the automobile represents an unattainable ideal, a self-contained unit that shelters, warms and cools in perfect comfort,

yet is also capable of high speeds thanks to a highly complex, and incredibly reliable, collection of mass-produced moving parts. A car, with about 10,000 different parts, can be designed from scratch in 15 months, manufactured in about 15 hours and then function perfectly, with only minor maintenance, for 15 years. Compared to buildings, with their slow and unwieldy construction process, their frequent woeful inefficiency and the difficulty of introducing an aesthetic approach that equates to a progressive modernity, it's little wonder many frustrated architects dabbled in car design. The history of the modernist automobile is rapidly becoming a vital coda to the work of major architects, usually presented in unchallenging homage to the cross-disciplinary skills of the great masters who could turn their hand to any form or machine they liked.

Le Corbusier's famous photo of the Villa Stein-de Monzie, Paris (1927) seems incongruous now. By virtue of the fast advancing state of vehicle technology, the Voisin 10 CV (Le Corbusier's own) standing before the Villa's pristine white geometry appears dated – a period piece. Ironically, the sloth-like progress of domestic architecture now gives the house itself a welcome sheen of novelty. Our homes might get smarter, crammed with communications technology and 'labour-saving' gadgets, yet these so-called smart homes still adhere to the traditional aesthetic of bricks and mortar, concealing their innovations behind a style that's little altered in over a century. In comparison, the motor car is happy to wear technology on its sleeve – its styling is an outward expression of confidence in the future.

Here is the heart of the problem – that it is the automobile, not architecture, that symbolises the age. Consumer awareness of different ages, styles, products, functions and desires ensures that the future is a relatively easy concept to conjure up, an amalgam of technology, styling and vision recognisably different from what's currently available. World's Fairs, International Exhibitions and auto shows all propagate rosy visions of a shortly-arriving technological paradise, with the car playing a central role. The concept car is an

unequalled futurist device, priming the buyer for innovation and new styling, whilst able to draw on the vast visual depository of the past to evoke almost any era, portrayed through the eyes of the present. There is a sense of continuity in car design, with significant changes from model to model made palatable by immediately perceptible nods to the original. Porsche, for example, make much capital of the physical lineage of their 996 model, lining up the company's products from the 1950s 356 all the way through to the latest machine. While each succeeding model is responding to the developments in aerodynamic technology, new materials and manufacturing processes that allow the design to be honed and improved, this technological evolution is represented physically through shapes which echo the styling of the past.

The automotive aesthetic hasn't always been hailed as forward thinking and progressive. The rococo fins of 1950s Detroit were bemoaned as vulgar ostentation by buttoned-up modernists and pilloried by consumer rights' champions as excessive and wasteful. Yet for the futurists, this was tomorrow made real. Car manufacturers made sure that the concept cars created for fairs and shows still bore references to the models in the showrooms. This form of styling found its architectural equivalent in Googie, the roadside ephemera epitomised by burger bars and drive-thrus. Googie was boldly coloured and strikingly shaped, architectural expressionism for the commercial age. Dynamic sculptural forms hailed the coming tomorrow, signalling complicity with the driver as he roared past in his softly-sprung, push-button automatic machine. The gulf between the geometric planes of International Modernism, or the serrated raw edges of New Brutalism, and the style's capacity for energetic vulgarity was broad. Googie was true carchitecture, expressive and unafraid to engage in a popular vocabulary, while remaining as transient and eye-catching as the annual model change.

Such physical manifestations of progress are anathema to the housing market. Here, external features – 'styling', if you will – signify longevity, solidity, tradition and permanence – the values expected of a home (not only by the buyer, but by the mortgage lender as well). Retrogressive design has a stranglehold on homebuilding. What we are now seeing is a similar willingness by the motor industry to plunder the past. Automobile manufacturers are increasingly adept at appropriating styling cues from the past in order to convey a sense of history, continuity and tradition. Retro in car design, as the industrial designer Richard Seymour says, is 'the pathology of inner-examination yielding symbolism, which found a voice in 1990s automotive production.' Yet as Seymour pointed out in *Domus* magazine, while manufacturers initially strove to emulate that which once made them great, what they are ultimately hoping to find it their 'authentic DNA', those elements of design which convey the essence of their brand without distilling technological progress and advance. Design studios such as those helmed by Freeman Thomas, responsible for the Audi TT, New Beetle (with J Mays) and the Dodge Super8 Hemi, or Frank Stephenson's knowing homage to Issigonis's Mini for BMW, create vehicles that carry an intrinsic understanding of a brand's history and visual language.

With this increased visual emphasis in mind, automobile manufacturers are starting to highlight the association between environmental design and automotive style. Frank Lloyd Wright, once quoted as saying that his 1940 Lincoln Continental was the most beautiful car in the world, has resurfaced in Lincoln publicity material to accompany the launch of their MK9 concept vehicle. Lincoln's new emphasis on 'American Luxury' approvingly quotes America's nurturing attitude towards modern design. 'The freedom of expression in America, and the youthful character and optimistic nature of Americans has produced truly influential designers and architects such as Charles Eames and Pierre Koenig,' claimed Lincoln design director Gerry McGovern, 'People such as Ludwig Mies van der Rohe, Le Corbusier and Eero Saarinen did some of their best work here.' The car, McGovern's argument implies, has segued seamlessly into our built environment, becoming just another facet of the urban realm.

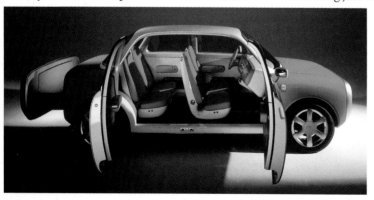

Left, above and opposite above: Though unlikely ever to be manufactured, Marc Newson's Ford 021C concept car was a brave move by the manufacturer as it deliberately crossed over into the world of product design. The 021C, a toy-like vehicle finished in bright orange or green, was paraded in fashion magazines and showcased at the Milan Furniture Fair. The interior, produced in conjunction with furniture manufacturers B&B Italia, eschewed hi-tech gadgetry for a reductivist feel, while the shelf-like boot contained a set of Prada-designed fitted luggage, sealing the car's designer reputation. Opposite below: Ford's StreetKa accentuates the popular Ka's youth appeal by adding elements of custom culture – wide track, large wheels and racing details. Intended as a concept car, it will soon enter production.

Given the prevalence of isolated, rural imagery in car advertising, recent Sports Utility Vehicle adverts have broken the mould. While there remains an emphasis on conquered nature, SUV advertising also uses hard-edged urban backgrounds and environments, all the better to suggest a cocoon-like enclosure against the real world. Current American models are unprecedented in their size and aggressive appearance. Isuzu's grotesque Axiom, its grille gawping like a basking shark, juts out of the page on a sea of wet tarmac. 'Resident non-conformist', reads the strap-line; this is urban street talk, not rural one-upmanship. Mercury's 2002 Mountaineer makes more explicit the link between the SUV and the city. Photographed against the concrete curves of Eero Saarinen's TWA Terminal at JFK Airport, the decidedly paunchy Mountaineer is billed as 'More Bauhaus than Bruiser'. Ignoring the mix-up of modern architectural movements, it's Mercury's claim that 'it may just be the first SUV designed not only to take on an environment, but to become an elegant extension of it' that sticks in the mind. The 'strong, urban-inspired exterior', shifted along by 239 horsepower (which will certainly take on *the* environment), is a coded way of selling intimidation, the raw commodity of the city. Cadillac advertise their new 2002 Escalade

(semiotically conjuring up images of freedom) against a backdrop of bunker-like buildings. The Escalade itself isn't unlike a small edifice, with vast headlights and a towering radiator reminiscent of a subway station vent shaft. With the option to check your email on the move – via GM's OnStar system of delivering navigation and information to the driver ('You're never alone with OnStar') – the Escalade approaches the status of mobile building.

What of the bucolic idyll, free from asphalt, road signs, restrictions and smog (not to mention other motorists) that has been harnessed to sell us cars since their conception? Cars might be literally costing us the earth, but study the aesthetics and typical environments of the automobile advert and you'd never suspect this was even an issue. Some clichés; empty, winding country lanes or highways; the only obstacles well-flagged and serving merely to illustrate superior braking power; cities filled with, alternatively, faceless clones longing to break out of their Identikit existences through the purchase of a shiny new car, or by a multi-cultural smorgasbord of happy, shiny people, their lives enriched by the presence of aforementioned vehicle; other cars, unidentifiable, grey, sludgy. It is ironic that the SUV should upend this tradition: a form of transport descended from

a countryside-conquering utility vehicle, it is now sold as a means of cosseting oneself from the rigours of everyday urban life.

As the SUV slips into our cities – mobile office and personal bunker – it becomes apparent that contemporary carchitecture is more likely to be manifested on the road than alongside it. The car is our primary point of reference for the appearance of the future. Architecture takes second place, cowed by the clashing demands of the motorist and the urbanist. Technological advance constantly lags behind the consumer perception of modern – generated through media imagery such as science fiction films and books and non-functioning styling prototypes. Our willingness to be seduced by the future is allowing the car to develop into more than mere mode of transport.

'We're deeply schizoid over whether our homes should be a point of entry for technology or a point of resistance. We fetishise the discrepancy, crazily dealing with it,' claimed the architectural historian Michael Sorkin in *Exquisite Corpse* (1994). Of course, the alternative is to take our technology with us. As Jane Holtz Kay observed:

'So it is that we spend our lives behind the wheel. With almost two motor vehicles for every [American] household, the car has become the ship of the highway desert. A multipurpose vessel, the automobile is outfitted to allay our hours sequestered there, a home away from home. The motor vehicle is a private chamber to telephone a buddy or boss with one hand and little concentration, a powder room to put on makeup, a cafeteria for lunching – at times simultaneously... Self-professed safe drivers take notes, talk to their clients, fight with their mates, or, incredibly, read or watch TV. Our backseats and trunks have become the attics of America.'

And it's true; sitting in our cars, bumper to bumper, traders have adapted their behaviour to target the stationary consumers; cars are a captive audience for newspaper vendors, flower sellers, squeegee merchants and other chancers. Inside, we're cosseted by every available technology, each transferring swiftly from their domestic setting to our new, mobile (most of the time) environment. Previous generations might have had to make do with thinly-sliced veneer picnic tables in the back of their Austin Vanden Plas, and perhaps a crackly wireless, but today we are likely to expect an in-car DVD, games systems, multi-speaker stereos, satellite navigation and more cup holders than it is physically possible to use.

New York University's Urban Research Initiative speculates that in the future cities will be dependent on the processing and circulation of information, not physical traffic. Many automobile manufacturers propose that their products will find a natural place within this information future, acting as mobile nodes, wandering plug-in storage points for vast amounts of information. The satellite navigation system, once the preserve of the geographically, though not financially, challenged is moving swiftly towards ubiquity on new cars. Nissan and Audi, amongst others, are pushing in-car DVD technology to control navigation and audio-visual systems, while Ford's 24/7 and Nissan's Chappo concept cars pitch themselves as 'living rooms on wheels', mobile technology centres complete with flexible seating, a raft of computer screens and all the accoutrements of the 1970s bachelor pad.

In this brave new world of fragmentation and specialisation, car makers have two choices – deny their 'car-ness' with 'one box' styling that shuns sleek lines in favour of space and flexibility, or create exaggerated, over-styled throwbacks that evoke the scale, nomenclature, appearance and prestige of a bygone era: Mercedes' Maybach and McLaren projects, Lincoln's MK9, new cars from Bristol, Bugatti and Bentley to name but a few. Today's drivers are less and less inclined – or able – to service their own cars, as heightened complexity puts off the amateur mechanic and automated warning systems monitor impending failure. The Audi A2, for example, hides its engine, with a flap at the front giving no clues as to the location of the power unit. Likewise, the independent roadside garage is confined to the suburbs. Instead, we have chain-owned, branded petrol stations, complete with lucrative sidelines in grocery items. Petrol

Left: Audi's TT began as a design study at the 1995 Frankfurt Motor Show. Its reception encouraged the company to turn the prototype into production reality, and the car – remarkably faithful to the original concept – debuted in 1998, with a roadster following two years later. Opposite: The Audi A2 (2000), seen in this press ad taking a turn around Steinmann & Schmid's iconic Parkhaus, builds on the company's well- marketed reputation for technical innovation with its all-aluminium body to cut fuel consumption. Above: The arrival of DaimlerChrysler's Smart car in 1997 was trailed by an equally smart media campaign by the Weber, Hodel, Schmid ad agency in Zürich. The car was introduced via the coded phrase 'reduce to the max', which appeared on mail-outs, websites and posters many months before the car was even unveiled.

is a loss leader. Pedestrians create the turnover.

Yet faith and technology remain optimistically linked, ill-starred lovers in a constant state of conflict. Manufacturers lure us into automobiles with interiors of ever-increasing quality, tactility and luxuriousness. Bel Geddes' radio wave navigation, dreamed up for Futurama in 1939, is now a production reality, albeit as the expensive Distronic option on the Mercedes CL, a radar-based cruise control that ensures you keep your distance from the car in front. Experiments with driverless cars continue.

The car is now the testing ground for nascent mobile internet services. In America, companies such as Wingcast are hoping to pipe the internet into the commuting nation. 'Car services are the mobile platform of the century', CEO Harel Kodesh was quoted as saying by *Wired* magazine. The automobile will become a portal – providing a information fixes of news, diary updates, as well as health, entertainment and shopping requirements, keeping commuters connected in their metal boxes. Current technologies, including General Motors' OnStar system, give the driver access to an operator who can activate functions remotely, such as opening cars when the keys are locked inside, provide breakdown assistance and medical advice. The internet-enabled car is a new futurist destination, an aspirational alteration of a mass-market technology to stimulate sales and demand.

In an age when 'design' is a commodity, it is ironic that manufacturers are closing ranks, merging and blending to maintain their profits. The complex ownership structures that characterise the industry have led to 'one platform'

solutions – engineering that encompasses a myriad of different territories and cultures, brands and models. Yet is our expectation of a model change every few years a result of the continual process of modernisation, or is it simply a response to our desire to see progress expressed through change and novelty? In the 1950s, the heyday of the annual model change, the new model bore the following year to ensure that consumers felt their technology was sufficiently advanced. 'The Big Three of Detroit were spending more than a billion dollars a year to put a new dress on their cars each year,' grumbled the anti-consumerist writer Vance Packard in *The Waste Makers* (1961), his seminal tract against Detroit's endless – and costly – emphasis on design 'evolution'. In hindsight, however, those 'new dresses' were shaping the future, a relentless, consumer-driven programme of constantly challenging visual awareness and perception.

In this brave new world of mobile, miniature architecture, nomenclature provides a crucial element. Interbrand Newell and Sorrell are one of many firms specialising in the intensely competitive and complex world of creating car names, researching copyright, potential cultural sensitivities and global meanings. The company's explanation of their work speaks volumes about how we continue to perceive the car as a force for good. 'Mondeo is coined from the Latin *mundus* meaning 'world', and was developed for Ford's first global car', explains their literature helpfully. Our responses to vehicles are now carefully conditioned. 'Carisma suggests personality, contributing to the distinctive brand presence

Even when British car manufacturing had reached its risible nadir in the mid-1970s, MG's sales brochures managed adeptly to appeal to lifestyle in an attempt to sell cars. The manufacturer's name, British Leyland, was already synonymous with disastrous build quality, and the copy line may have been embarrassingly weak (where *does* it matter most, and where, by implication, does it not matter?), but the photographs press all the right buttons for an upwardly-mobile bachelor of the era. He's the one at the wheel of course, the thick moustache firmly set to indicate nonchalance and control. Beside him, the woman allows herself a knowing grin. In another image, the MG finds itself in the unlikely role of poolside guest at that perfect index of middle class sophistication: the summer barbecue. Again, although hiding demurely behind the yukka plant, the man is in charge.

**Where it matters most, it takes a lot to beat an MGB**

Where looks matter, it's difficult to believe it's a hard-working 2+2.

Certainly, the classic sports car styling gives nothing away.

But built into those stylish curves are features that make it a very desirable sports saloon.

The opening tailgate opens up to approximately 9·6 cubic feet of luggage space.

The tinted heat-absorbent glass cools down the interior and the opening rear side windows freshen it up.

And superb suspension means even better ride and handling than ever before.

It's also as conscious of your family's safety as you are.

With 5 mph impact-absorbing bumpers, hazard warning lights and halogen headlights.

There's also fitted head restraints, inertia reel seat belts, reversing lamps, laminated windscreen and a heated rear window.

It's economical too: with overdrive as standard.

Which means you can expect good fuel consumption even when cruising at high speed.

All this, yet the body shape and radial-shod Rostyle wheels hint at power and acceleration in safety.

It's this combination that makes the MGB GT hard to beat.

Launched in 1969 just two months after the US put men on the moon, and the same year that Concorde first flew, the Fiat 128 was a dreadfully boring, boxy design by comparison with its space age contemporaries. But the modest mid-sized Fiat at least brought front wheel drive to the small car market. Its stubby exterior was mirrored by a modern, 'oversquare' engine typical of Italian cars. It positively loved being driven at screaming-pitch, foot to the floor, hand on horn, heart in mouth. Odd then, that the company's chosen environment for its marketing photograph was this lazy suburban garden, complete with an elegant hippie chick who might surely expect to drive something a little, well, cooler. Worse, the car ushered in the damaging era of the Italian rust-bucket. It was a popular model however, with total sales reaching 3 million.

of Mitsubishi's popular saloon,' while 'Vitara is taken from the Latin *vita*, meaning life, and suggests all the energy and fun associated with off-roading' and 'Vectra is coined from the hi-tech term *vector*, suggesting movement and direction.' While tales of misnomers, mistakes and misunderstanding have acquired the status of urban legend (that Nova, in Spanish, means 'doesn't go', for example. Or the oft-repeated tale of the Mitsubishi Starion, a Japanese car that was intended to have a more equine name – and came complete with prancing horse badge – before a particular trait of Japanese pronunciation came to the fore), successful names enter our language unquestioned. Failures are immensely costly, alienating market shares, even whole populations.

Perhaps automotive novelty has its place. By comparison, the names for new housing make depressing reading. The 'Arran', 'Bromley', 'Coniston', 'Earlsford', 'Fairford', 'Sherbourne', 'Stretton' and 'Stamford' (all from volume homebuilder Bryant Homes), evoke a debilitated image of Constable Country – haywains and haystacks, a rural idyll that we can't reach via non-existent public transport, a wilderness that can only be tamed by our cars. It wasn't always this way. Attempts to mass-market a domestic futurism comparable with the car occurred periodically throughout the 20th century. London's annual Ideal Home Show, now a symbol of the reactionary stasis that infects domestic architecture, popularised concept houses that, like concept cars, introduced new domestic technology and styles. Alison and Peter Smithson's 1956 contribution was perhaps the most radical in the show's history. Their 'House of the Future' came complete with a curved, plastic interior, integral cupboards, Nylon-clothed models and a wagon-load of technology. The Smithsons' vision created a template for the future, yet perversely had little effect. Naturally, the house included a car, a be-finned, bulbous creation best described as Dagenham Detroit.

The Smithsons also had a love affair with the Citroën DS, setting in motion what has perhaps become an architectural cliché. 'Cancel your own indicators' read a small ad in the back of *Building*

*Design*, promising quirkiness, individuality and design integrity – every architect's private self-image. Alison Smithson went further, creating *AS in DS*, a seminal book shaped in homage to the DS's teardrop floor-pan (elegant and functional on the road, unsurprisingly awkward as page design). *AS in DS* charted the couple's frequent travels from London to Wiltshire, a journey captured through fleeting glimpses, sketches and photography.

The DS continues to inspire creative passion amongst members of the architectural community, providing a clue as to the architectural perception of the automobile's role in society. The DS, a revolutionary shape famously extolled by Roland Barthes as reminiscent of the great medieval gothic cathedrals, was a generational leap in terms of styling and technology. Yet despite the car's popularity, and the company's determined attempts to plough a similar aesthetic and technological furrow with the subsequent SM, GS, CX and, to a smaller extent, XM models, the DS has come to symbolise quirky individuality, rather than cutting edge futurism. In other words, it was misunderstood. It's not hard to see how modern architects might identify with such a symbol: this is what we could all be driving, were it not for the muddle-headed masses. Popular rejection of the aesthetic of domestic modernist architecture was a similar slight; the DS represents an adherence to a future that never came to fruition. Instead, we chose to make cars our totems of modernity, leaving domestic architecture far behind.

The megastructural visions, vast engineering projects, motorway intersections, car parks and off-ramps, remain the purest expressions of carchitecture. Today, auto-centric design has shifted from architecture to the car itself, not only the most technologically advanced possession we own, but also the most highly styled item. Cars are the most accessible 'design' object most people ever see, with new models defining our environment and shaping the way we see and perceive the future – far more so than the visions provided by architects. The carchitecture of the future will be the environments we drive, not the environments we drive through.

# PARK AND GLIDE: THE FUTURE CITY

LIZ BAILEY

Architects, planners and city dwellers have long dreamt of having the means to compress the metropolis into a swiftly traversable area, by making travel fast, easy, cheap and virtually instantaneous. While the coming of the car heralded much promise, the grimy reality has dimmed the ardour of even the most committed autophile.

When rumours about a miracle transportation technology began to circulate on internet bulletin boards at the start of 2001, most commentators retained a sufficiently critical view of technology's abilities to make sweeping societal changes. Yet in the face of the hyperbole, others were quick to hail the sketchy proposals as revolutionary. Initially known, mysteriously, as IT, the new mode of transport swiftly acquired a more universal nickname: Ginger.

What is IT? Initial research into the claims indicates that IT is a scooter-esque mode of personal transport with an engine that runs, apparently, on hydrogen. So IT is effectively emission-free – its only byproduct is that well-known environmentally friendly non-pollutant, H2O. Nearly everyone who has heard of IT is running around saying, 'I've just gotta have IT.' Unfortunately, IT's inventor isn't talking about it. Naturally,

the online community has done little else: what will IT mean to us if IT in fact goes into production? Will IT really mean redesigning and re-regulating our cities' transport infrastructure, and if so, how? Are we really ready for IT?

IT/Ginger's creator, Dean Kamen, is to all appearances an angry young(ish) inventor of everything from insulin-delivery systems to all-terrain wheelchairs. Kamen craves the sort of celebrity US society accords to actors and athletes but not, he fumed at a recent conference, to thinkers. In presenting Ginger to the world, however, he certainly managed to stir up the kind of media attention usually reserved for Hollywood divorces and scandals, and all by using just one author and a teasing ten-minute presentation. Aside from this, Kamen has been decidedly cagey about the whole project, holding only the one actual publicity stunt showing a glimpse of Ginger to a favoured few in a hotel room last December. Using 'a few spanners', Kamen snapped two Gingers together in about ten minutes before a select audience of high-profile hi-tech company heads, including Apple CEO Steve Jobs, Amazon.com founder Jeff Bezos and Silicon Valley *über* venture capitalist John Doerr. *New Scientist* reported Jobs as saying 'If enough people see the

machine, you won't have to convince them to architect cities around it. It'll just happen'. Kamen merely complained that the comment was taken out of context.

Possibly Kamen's most powerful public relations tool though was us, the public. Or, to be more specific, the initial response, which seemed to indicate that Ginger really *was* what we had been waiting for. The answer to the dissatisfaction and disaffection with current urban transport arrangements that would appear to span the globe. The hyper-hype surrounding Ginger reached its zenith when Harvard Business School Press agreed to pay journalist Steve Kemper US$250,000 for a book about Ginger, before either the publisher or Kemper's agent (or anyone else) actually knew what it was or how – or even if – IT would work. The very keen, including *Inside Magazine* reporter Adam Penenberg and The Smoking Gun website, had managed to glean more snippets about IT by trawling through trademark and patent filings using US Trademark Electronic Search System (TESS), domain and company name registrations, financial transactions and factory blueprints, all available under the US Freedom of Information Act.

In early March 2001, Penenberg reported his findings and The Smoking Gun posted a set of patent

drawings. Speculation on the nature of Kamen's 'personal mobility' project had reached fever pitch: it would run on hydrogen; it would use a 'dynamic stabilisation' system that mimics the way upright human beings maintain their balance, similar to the one Kamen had developed for IBOT, his untippable motorised wheelchair.

Although these investigations revealed something of Kamen's activities, they told nothing of his actual intentions. Even after the stunt with the wrenches, the world was still waiting for that information. At time of publication, knowledge of Ginger consisted of the following (uncertain) facts: IT is a light, balancing vehicle that lets you stand upright easily, has an engine that produces only a few drops of water and may cost less than US$2,000. And make no mistake – the engine technology is very real. It's what is known as a Stirling engine. America's Stirling Engine Society describes the propulsion unit as 'an extra-lean, low pollution output engine'. Because the Stirling engine uses external combustion – i.e. heat from outside the engine – to move its pistons, it avoids creating pollutants and can operate equally well on any of a number of types of fuel: natural gas, propane, alcohol, petrol, diesel, and of course hydrogen – even solar

Above: Among the only clues about a mysterious and supposedly revolutionary new 'personal mobility vehicle' known as IT are a few sketches lodged with the US patent office. Left: The much-maligned Sinclair C5, launched in the UK in 1985, was developed as an eco-friendly personal vehicle. But only 12,000 were ever sold, and most of those were foreign sales after the company had folded.

Opposite top: Kevin Inkster's Airboard 2000, a personal hover-craft with a top speed of 15mph, featured in the opening ceremony of the 2000 Olympics in Sydney.

power. Using heat to create motion also means Stirling engines are 'extra quiet'.

Yet what draws us to Ginger is not just IT's lightness and cheapness and greenness and quietness or even necessarily the real-ness of the science behind it. Ginger holds the promise of letting us shake up the existing transport order, a means of attaining urban utopia. Subsequent previews of Kemper's book proposal have revealed slightly more. According to P J Mark's article on Inside.com, the proposal describes IT as something that will 'sweep over the world and change lives, cities, and ways of thinking'. Kemper's proposal sheds some light on the way Ginger's core technology might wreak havoc on both industry and government. It will 'have a big, broad impact not only on social institutions but some billion-dollar old-line companies' – Kamen's words à la Kemper. Ginger will 'profoundly affect our environment and the way people live worldwide. It will be an alternative to products that are dirty, expensive, sometimes dangerous and often frustrating, especially for people in the cities.' IT, says Kemper, will be a mass-market consumer product 'likely to run afoul of existing regulations and or inspire new ones', probably requiring 'meeting with city planners, regulators, legislators, large commercial companies and university presidents about how cities, companies and campuses can be retro-fitted for Ginger'.

Who among us does not love the idea of distressing big companies? In *Who Framed Roger Rabbit?*, automobile tyre manufacturers deliberately put Los Angeles' Red Car trolleys out of business. The film's plot is conspiracy theory mythology at its best, but certainly big car makers are truculent and unenthusiastic about, for instance, French engineer Guy Nègre's compressed-air cars (www.zeropollution.com).

Conspiracy theorists the world over thrill to tales of ultra-efficient engines being hushed up by the big oil companies, their inventors hounded and pursued until they forfeit their dreams.

The Net has buzzed with public responses to Ginger ranging from fury – why isn't Kamen simply releasing into the public domain something which would so obviously benefit mankind? – to delight and parody. Such public deliberations give the flavour of the sorts of regulatory debates we might see if – or when? – Ginger becomes widely available: 'Seriously, this is so dangerous I can't see it ever happening,' writes someone billed only as y6y6y6 on www.metafilter.com. 'Even if cities build around it, a private roadway filled with these things would be a roller derby. If it goes over 20mph it's too fast to be safe. If it goes under 20mph it's too slow to replace the bike.' 'Plus,' adds y6y6y6, 'once people get really fat because they don't have to walk any more these will start using up too much power.' The power question has already begun to exercise big business: Adam Penenberg reports that Ford, DaimlerChrysler and GM all plan next year to market 'hybrid fuel-cell vehicles that change gas into hydrogen, dramatically cutting down on emissions'.

Penenberg points out that

a hydrogen-powered scooter is a logical 'technological first step' towards cars based on this same principle. But despite Texaco, Shell, BP Amoco and Exxon Mobil all working on hydrogen projects, he says, the word on the street is pure hydrogen fuel-cell vehicles will not become widespread before 2010. Ginger is not, by a very long shot, the only attempt at a low-pollution or revolutionary transport solutions, or even the most intriguing. Guy Nègre and his son Cyril are gearing up to produce their compressed-air powered cars for taxi fleets in Mexico and elsewhere. Toyota has developed the green-but-hideous Prius, with its hybrid petrol-electric engine, and Honda's Insight also represents a (less advanced) take on the hybrid system. However, these technologies still require government and manufacturer subsidies to survive in the market place, negating their many advantages. For the dedicated futurist, the sky is no longer even the limit: those who have really reached the end of their public transport tether can opt for a Backpack Helicopter (£25,000) or Solo Trek VTOL (vertical take-off and landing vehicle, £60,000, both from www.gadgetmasters.com), or wait for Robert Moller's Skycar (www.moller.com).

But out of all of these real, imaginary and hopeful solutions, Ginger avoids being either too

sandal-wearing-ecowarrior, or just too damn James Bond. IT is not only possible and probable, IT has also somehow tugged most effectively at the techno-obsessed community's heart strings. Perhaps Ginger is simply the right idea at the right time. Just over a century of the traffic jam, agonisingly slow buses, disappearing trams and trolleys, and badly run subway-metro-undergrounds has left many of us not only frustrated and angry with our travel needs unsatisfied, but frightened at our lack of control over our own day-to-day destiny. IT – which some speculate stands for 'individual transport' – could be the Robin Hood of its day: wresting power back from the state and returning it to the people.

The dubious reaction to Ginger is of course nothing new. Historically, new technologies have come under fire from people and governments for a multitude of reasons – safety, expense, control. The visionary dreams of futurists from the seventeenth century onwards, with their focus on personal flying machines and unlimited energy sources, linger in the minds of the sceptics; we've been here before. Having shaped our cities to accommodate the automobile – a technology that promised so much and continues to be a central focus of our culture – would civic authorities be willing to start again from scratch?

Since 1963, engineer Robert Moller has devoted his life to developing the Skycar. With early 'saucer' models like the M200X (left), designed and flown in the 1980s, to the latest, the M400 (above), Moller has tried to be first into a market fraught with potential problems. The computer-controlled M400, with a $1 million price tag, will take off vertically, using eight tilting rotary engines to provide lift, thrust and a projected top speed of nearly 400mph. Moller is currently seeking vital Federal Aviation Authority certification, a process that has already consumed ten years.

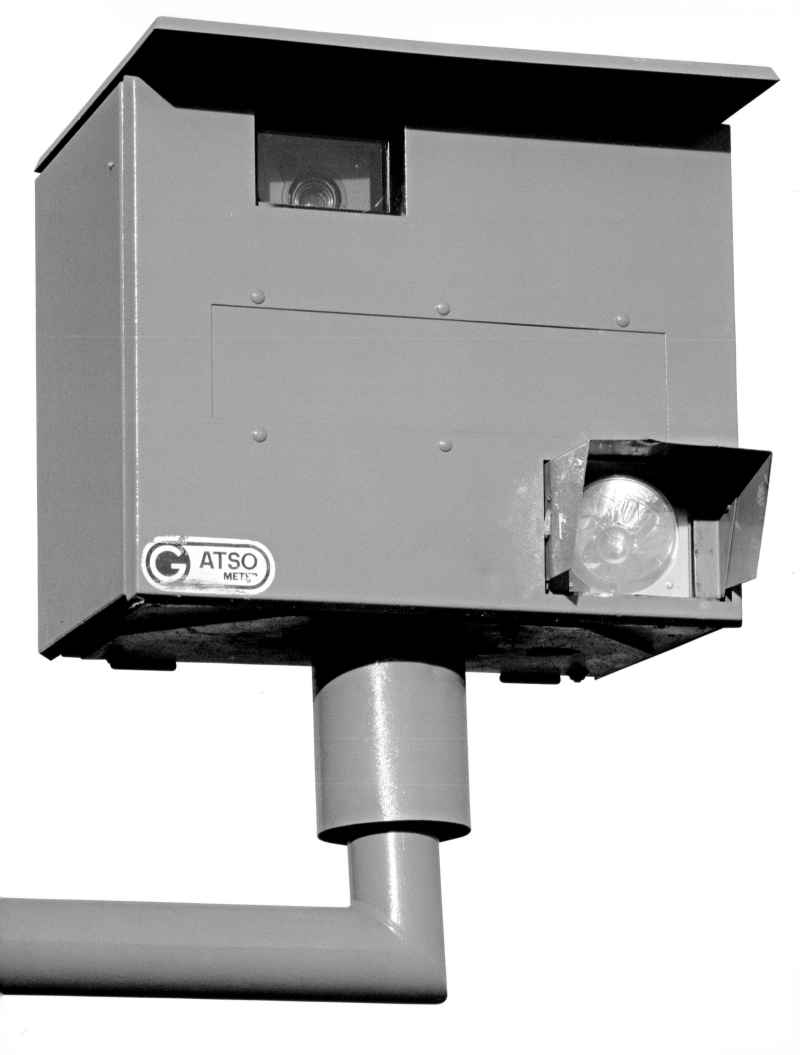

# THE WESTWAY: A ROAD TOO FAR

SANDY McCREERY

'Our own apartment house at Drayton Park stood a mile to the north of the airport in a pleasant island of modern housing units, landscaped filling stations and supermarkets, shielded from the distant bulk of London by an access spur of the northern circular motorway which flowed past us on its elegant concrete pillars. I gazed down at this immense motion sculpture, whose traffic deck seemed almost higher than the balcony rail against which I leaned. I began to orientate myself again round its reassuring bulk, its familiar perspectives of speed, purpose and direction.'

J.G.Ballard, *Crash*, (1973)

It does not take any great insight to recognise that roads constitute a significant proportion of the built environment, nor that the use of motor vehicles on them has brought about extraordinary social change. Architects have seen this, and several canonical Modernists, such as Le Corbusier, Louis Kahn, and Alison & Peter Smithson devoted considerable attention to their design. But it seems that architectural historians and cultural theorists have been remarkably blind to the issues raised by roads. For example, the work of theorists such as David Harvey and Henri Lefebvre consistently examines the re-configurations of socio-cultural space, yet almost never gives specific attention to the role played by roads. For if we accept that architecture and culture are socially produced, how could one fail to conclude that roads, those great conduits of social transformation, must have strong relationships with architectural and cultural practice? Indeed we could argue that the architecture of the twentieth century cannot be fully understood without recognising the social effects of roads built for motor vehicles. In order to start interpreting the cultural significance of roads, this essay looks at the circumstances surrounding the construction of the Westway; the elevated motorway, opened in 1970, that runs westwards through North Kensington from the Marylebone Road in central London.

Now on one level, historical materialism can provide a rather tidy reading of roads; they are instruments of social control and have been used as such since at least Roman times. They have both served and symbolised flows of power. The *Art and Power* exhibition at London's Hayward Gallery in 1995 took trouble to highlight how the first motorways were built, and exploited in terms of propaganda, by the militaristic regimes of Hitler and Mussolini. Cultural historians have begun to give increasing attention to the use of processions, notably on the new roads of sixteenth century Rome, to direct people's minds as well as their feet. The argument linking the 'strategic beautification' of Haussmann's boulevards with the social and cultural transformation of nineteenth century Paris has now been rehearsed so many times that

The twin decks of London's A40 urban motorway, built to carry citizens quickly out of the grim city centre. Riding high on the upper deck affords drivers some of the finest views of West London, but beneath the main carriageway the quality of urban space has been consistently poor. Photograph: Alex de Rijke

it has begun to acquire the status of truth.

But such cases lend themselves readily to a social-power based analysis; it is generally clear who holds the whiphand, who is controlling whom. The same cannot be said for the urban motorways of late twentieth century Western democracies, such as the Westway. In this contemporary context power is overwhelmingly mediated through money, not force, and its machinations less overt. With private motorised transport now an option for increasing numbers of people, it becomes much harder to pinpoint who exactly are the winners, and who the losers. It seems that we all, in different and complex configurations, experience both benefits and drawbacks. And it would be simplistic, if not simply wrong, to argue that the capitalist is necessarily the winner: several of the world's wealthiest nations have built relatively few motorways – for example the Netherlands, Denmark and Sweden – and Doncaster (on the A1(M) motorway) is no boom-town. Indeed there are those who argue quite forcefully against there being any direct connection between road-building and economic development.

Now I believe that road-building does serve capitalism, but that the means are cultural at least as much as they are economic, and it is the ideological superstructure that I wish to give attention to here. Roads change the cultural basis of society, and in doing so they pave the way for a deepening of capitalist economic relations. Building a road does not, in itself, make you rich (indeed it may well make you poorer). But it is the socio-spatial and cultural changes that appear to inevitably follow that render a place unable to resist further intensification of capitalism. By looking at the cultural and political ideology that has surrounded road-building (particularly in Britain) since the Second World War, through the concept of the opposed paradigms, the Village and the Metropolis, we can gain a better understanding of the how roads infuse culture.

The Village and the Metropolis have been fundamental to the discourse of social space formation. These are, precisely, representations, intellectual constructs that have no real place outside the mind, although in the Lefebvrian manner they relate to the lived experience of concrete space. Within capitalism we can conceive of the Village as essentially defensive, a space of resistance, and the Metropolis as invasive. As notions they have a tenuous relationship with Lefebvre's understanding of appropriated and dominated space. I believe that the Metropolis has been of immense service to the continuing intensification of capitalism, and driving along the Westway is one of the most Metropolitan experiences available in London.

The Westway was planned by the London County Council, who claimed to be responding to a scientific analysis of the transport needs of Londoners. Their 1951 County of London Development Plan, in which the motorway was first proposed, identified two priorities: roads to alleviate congestion in the central area between Marble Arch and Aldgate, and roads to improve orbital circulation. Yet, as a radial route outside the centre, the Westway met neither of these criteria. Indeed it could only encourage more commuter cars into the congested centre, whilst at the same time exposing London's economy to increased competition from out-lying areas.

The Westway was not a response to existing needs, it was a response to a vision of a new kind of urban society – a Metropolitan vision. This notion of the Metropolis can be traced back to the mid-nineteenth century, as it is implicit within Baudelaire's conception of the *flâneur*. Baudelaire took the anonymous urban crowd as a positive metaphor of the urban condition. Modernists came to celebrate the urban experience for its freedom from social relations, even if they might regret the extent to which culture had become objectified.

Much of the excitement, and much of the threat, of the city came from the possibility of autonomous, sexually-charged, social encounters. The inevitable emotional detachment of the urban experience, the separation of lust from love, allowed a new control over desire. One has a degree of mastery over the individual reduced to a body, a detached object of pleasure. The Metropolis is

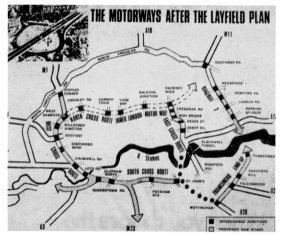

THE MOTORWAYS AFTER THE LAYFIELD PLAN

sexy precisely because it is reified. This conflation of subject and object was exploited for its sexual interest by image-makers throughout the twentieth century, whether we think of the soft curves of motor car styling, or Madonna's mechanistic basque and 'boy toys'.

A distinguishing feature of modern urban life, and one which contributed enormously to its liberating alienation, has been the control of space and time, or speed. When seeking to explain why young boys enjoyed fantasies of becoming train drivers, Freud in *Infantile Sexuality*, suggested it derived from the combination of fear and mechanical agitation. In the motor age, I suspect that it has more to do with control. Vehicles respond on demand, they do not answer back, they offer instant gratification, they provide a spectacle of individual control. In the Metropolis you may be isolated and intimidated, but you can also be mobile, independent, sexually-aware, in control.

The Metropolis makes it possible for the heroic architect to stand apart from society. This outlook was evident in Le Corbusier's detached perspectives; only the privileged master-planner could have enjoyed his views. And these were exactly the viewpoints adopted in the London County Council's rendering of the proposed Westway: high vantage points overlooking the swooping concrete curves. Indeed, most of the architectural and planning imagery of the Metropolitan ideal in Britain derives from Le Corbusier. In their influential 'Cluster City'

'The new mechanical speeds have disrupted the urban environment, creating permanent danger, causing traffic jams and paralysing communications, and interfering with hygiene. Mechanical vehicles ought to be agents of liberation and, through their speed, to bring about a valuable gaining of time. But their accumulation and their concentration at certain points have become both an obstacle to movement and the source of constant danger. Moreover, they have introduced into urban life numerous factors injurious to health. Their combustion gases spread in the air are harmful to the lungs and their noises induces in man a condition of permanent nervous irritability. The speeds that are now available

Opposite: The Layfield plan of 1973 was the compromise which followed the public enquiry into the Greater London Development Plan proposing three ring motorways for the city. Although the Tory Greater London Council of the day intended to build these cross routes, Labour won the next GLC election on a pledge to drop the scheme.
Opposite below: Le Corbusier's 1929 sketch of Rio.
Below: In these publicity drawings from the 1960s, the Westway is presented in all its pre-construction glory: the urban motorway as catalyst for utopia.

essay of 1957, the Smithson's quoted Le Corbusier: 'when night intervened the passage of cars along the autostrada traces luminous tracks that are like the trails of meteors flashing across the summer heavens'. They went on to acknowledge that 'we still respond to this dream', of people as shining objects speeding through space. And they were not alone. So too did the many city planning departments that sought to recreate the scene, particularly during the 1960s.

The economic basis of Le Corbusier's vision was a massive increase in the consumption of personal motorised transport. This, of course, was an enormously attractive proposition to capitalists, and it is no surprise that Le Corbusier received the funding to prepare his early schemes from car manufacturers. However, it is worth our remembering, although town-planners of the 1960s tended to forget, that he actually sought to reconcile the Metropolis with the Village. His schemes of the 1920s did not envisage that all citizens would become motorised. For example, his *Contemporary City for Three Million People* proposed an inner-core of one million motorised people, surrounded by workers' garden city communities, housing two million. Eventually his motorised citizens would be housed in his floating urban co-operative communities, the *unités*. But the need for Le Corbusier's schemes to be applied in total if the Village was to provide a brake to the increasing alienation of urban life was apparently lost on the London County Council planners.

Le Corbusier's image was forty years old before the construction of the Westway. This delay could be explained solely in terms of economic and political conditions; that Britain's economy had been limping through depression and war until 1960. Then Ernest Marples, whose family fortune came from civil engineering, was appointed Conservative Minister of State for Transport. He was able to promote Le Corbusier's vision with the aid of research showing that 60% of car owners voted Conservative, whereas only 11% voted Labour. The image was also attractive to the Labour opposition, who throughout the late 1950s and early 1960s repeatedly attacked the Government for not supporting Britain's most important industry – motor manufacturing.

But this can only be a partial explanation. The car industry did not suddenly become important in 1960, nor did motorists suddenly decide to vote Conservative. If the motor industry was crucial to the British economy, then why was road building not prioritised more in 1945? My view is that it was largely because of the continuing strength in planning discourse of the notion of the Village.

Conceiving the Village as the model of a cohesive, stable, supportive community has a long tradition in British architectural and social thought stretching back to Ruskin and Morris. For them,

**arouse the temptation to daily escape, far away, into nature, spread the taste for a mobility without restraint or measure and favour ways of life which, by breaking up the family, profoundly disturb the foundations of society. They condemn men to spend exhausting hours in all sorts of vehicles and little by little to lose the exercise of the healthiest and most natural of all functions: walking.'**
**CIAM: Charter of Athens: tenets, 1933, set out by Le Corbusier**

medieval (and pre-capitalist) rural communities offered the antidote to social fragmentation. Even if they did not use such language, the Village was the arena in which unalienated dwelling remained possible. Ebenezer Howard's interpretation in *Garden Cities of Tomorrow* makes it clear that he saw the communal ownership of land as a means of keeping capitalism at bay, preventing private interests taking precedence over those of the collective. This notion of the Village was particularly potent immediately after the Second World War, which helped foster a dominant little-Britain Village mentality.

By way of an illustration, The Exhibition of Architecture at the 1951 Festival of Britain was intended to demonstrate how science and planning, epitomised by the 1943 *County of London Plan*, would transform Britain's cities. That plan had in fact listed traffic congestion as the number one problem needing solution, yet this was totally played-down at the festival. The exhibit consisted of an area of the bombed East End that had been partially rebuilt as, to use their contemporary description, the 'neighbourhood of Lansbury'. The accompanying catalogue, the 'Guide to the Exhibition of Architecture, Town-planning and Building Research', focused consistently on the notion of the Village:

'London has grown in a sprawling fashion, gradually swallowing up the surrounding villages and open fields, and replacing them by drab suburbs with ill-defined boundaries. In spite of this, recognisable communities still survive with strong local loyalties.

A sense of community, of neighbourly responsibility, satisfies an essential human need. the underlying purpose of the Plan was to encourage this sense and stimulate or revive these communities and loyalties.'

This is the Village versus the Metropolis. This is why they chose to exhibit lived-in buildings. Lansbury was intended to be a scientifically planned Village community. It may well be numbingly dull architecturally, but it was the human subjects on display, not the architectural

'The city of speed is the city of success.'
Le Corbusier, *Guiding Principles of Town Planning*, 1925

objects. Needless to say, there were no major new roads at Lansbury.

Yet communities that convey a sense of the Village can be an attractive option to capitalists when built from scratch, on new sites, introducing entirely new places and patterns of consumption, and the New Towns policy was pursued with vigour after the second world war. But existing communities, particularly in urban areas where home ownership remained comparatively low, were noticeably resistant to any intensification of capitalism. If capitalism was to continue to find arenas for expansion in 1960 after the initial post-war rebuilding, then it needed to penetrate such places. Road building, usually combined with comprehensive slum clearance schemes (as urban roads will always be routed through the poorer areas of town), were to provide the solution.

Urban motorways are not effective simply because they destroy the fabric of existing social spaces, but because they introduce a new culture; a reified Metropolitan culture, which Modernism had rendered attractive, and that produces a deepening demand for capitalism's products. Roads are not dominant space just because they dominate their social surroundings, but also because they provide the arena in which the spectacle of commodity domination is performed.

Probably nowhere is the experience of reified culture more intense than on an urban motorway. We may have a deeply satisfying relationship with our car, but we cannot engage in spontaneous social interaction, nor can we walk, stop, get drunk, or be one of the millions excluded from using motor vehicles for a host of reasons. We can only go where the road takes us, at the pace it dictates. And yet modernism projected these as the great symbols of Metropolitan freedom – the freedom they actually offer is from the notion of the Village. There are no new destinations, only re-packaged ones. But along the way, many of the social spaces in which the unfolding contest between the Metropolis and the Village was actually lived, have been destroyed.

Roads have been uniquely successful in assisting capitalism. In the mid-1980s it was estimated that

Long abandoned, this
transport maintenance
depot in Paddington,
London, is now enjoying
a new lease of life as the
headquarters of fashion
retailer Monsoon.
Refurbished by AHMM,
Bicknell and Hamilton's
1965 concoction of
modernism and brutalism
directly overlooks the
motorway, cars streaming
past the strip windows,
the road brought into
the building.

Just as wildlife flourishes in the dead zones of urban infill – railway sidings, empty lots, abandoned housing and traffic islands – so roads create their own social ecosystems. These 'spaces between' litter the contemporary city, victims of planning shortfalls, truncated thinking and a surfeit of ideas.

London, like any major city, contains many such spaces, such as this narrow 'V' delineated by the winding Westway and the tracks of the tube line out of Ladbroke Grove station. In the distance hovers Trellick Tower, Ernö Goldfinger's freshly fashionable brutalist high-rise, its view of the road forming a key part of the building's urban appeal. The crammed railway arches are testament to the industry and activity that the railway brought – despite the blight inflicted by the tracks, new spaces were created and swiftly colonised. In contrast, the Westway's mostly empty undercroft signals missed opportunities.

The Westway's disregard for the existing street pattern is indicated by the jagged edges of estates and streets, bisected as the new road ploughed west to freedom. A brash industrial estate has been joined by a bland housing development. Not a single window acknowledges the road, just metres away from the red-tiled roofs.

Once built, the sleek carriageway of the publicity drawings failed to live up to the ideal – roads on stilts can only soar if they rise above and cross over, not form barriers and impediments. Yet looking at the wide skies and traffic-less vistas of the drawings, it's clear that the last thing the modernist master planners wanted was day-care centres, garages and storage units choking their willowy *pilotis* and grounding the road in everyday mundanity.

The Westway remains half-integrated, a mixture of elegant, panorama-rich futuristic flyover and ground-hugging concrete wall, bringing blight and inconvenience. Its ambitions were huge – witness the stubby fingers that still project from the north side of the White City roundabout, awaiting a future handshake with a road that never came. Flawed ambition isn't always an attractive quality, yet like Trellick Tower, the Westway has gradually crept into our affections, not just for its single-minded brutality and reminder of the ambitions of a bygone era, but also for its ability to provide us with a sensation so rare in the contemporary city – speed.

In 1970, George Clark and John O'Malley were the key figures behind a high-profile piece of urban activism, when North Kensington locals went up against the local council and its road builders in one of London's earliest anti-road protests.

as much as a half of the world's measured economic activity may be concerned with the making, fuelling and maintenance of motor vehicles. But it is their unseen role in consistently deepening the reification of culture that is most powerful. As the spaces of social relations are broken down, so our need to live our emotional lives through commodities increases.

A collision occurred at the Westway in 1970, when a dominant space of capitalism ran into a resistant urban community. The principal activists were George Clark and John O'Malley, both of whom were members of the London New Left Club. One can only speculate as to what informed their actions; certainly there are striking parallels between what happened in North Kensington and the ideas of the radical French Left, particularly those of Henri Lefebvre and the Situationist International. Clark and O'Malley encouraged the appropriation of space through the production of art works and street festivals. They were also particularly concerned to appropriate play space, and scored a notable success with a series of mass trespasses into Powis Square, a private square closed to the public, which forced the council to buy it for a children's play area. These were model tactics of the French Left, who valued play as an area of unalienated activity which could lead to personal, and therefore political, awakening.

The Westway conflict also originally centred around play space which the local community, again with O'Malley's encouragement, had appropriated under the flyover. It was when the contractors tried to seal the undercroft with concrete walls to create commuter car parks,

that the battle erupted. The North Kensington Play Space Group, led by O'Malley, scored the first success against the road-builders by pointing out the council had not granted itself planning permission for these car parks, giving them the legal means to delay construction. After six weeks the council capitulated entirely and conceded that the space beneath the road should be used for community purposes, even though only the vaguest of plans were being proposed. It is safe to assume that free market capitalism would otherwise have been unlikely to provide the horse-riding stables, sports centre, studio spaces, playgrounds and covered market that are to be found under the Westway today. We can understand this as a concrete synthesis between the Metropolis and the Village.

But regarding the other aspect to the conflict, housing, there appears to have been no such reconciliation. Clarke and O'Malley mounted an extremely effective publicity campaign that ran off the back of the London County Council's own promotion of the road. Many locals were eventually re-housed, yet their community was demolished and the motorway remains. True, the Greater London Council was consequently forced to abandon the planned massive construction of elevated motorways in inner London, but new motorways continue to arrive, such as the M11 extension in East London.

Capitalism has continued to intensify along the Westway corridor. Large areas around Western Avenue, the Westway's continuation, have recently gone through rapid re-shaping dedicated to motorised passive consumption. Probably nowhere else around London so closely resembles a North American 'Edge City'. The road itself was, until very recently, scheduled to be widened. This has already involved the demolition of part of the Wormholt estate, a model 1920s Village development of 'homes fit for heroes'. To walk by today, the sense of loss, both in terms of social space and social time, can be overwhelming. This is now a placeless, memory-less, social void. But to speed by, and up on to the Westway, that is to be in control. Or is it?

# 3. DRIVEN TO DISTRACTION

The predicament is that while we want the best of both worlds, the mechanical and the biological, nothing will stop us achieving the first at the cost of the second. Man has two passions behind this: the first is to increase his own mobility, the second is to live up to his neighbour. While happiness may be in his own garden, he will rarely believe it is not somewhere else where his car can now take him; and we must assume, therefore (and beyond possible doubt), that short of economic catastrophe or further intervention, the car is with us indefinitely.'

Geoffrey Jellicoe, *Motopia*, (1961)

Opposite above and previous pages: Led by campaign group Reclaim the Streets, up to 20,000 people took part in anti-road protests in London on 12 April 1997, ending up in Trafalgar Square. Sir Norman Foster's plans for pedestrianising the square were approved a year later, but still remain on hold. Opposite below: Building work on the controversial Newbury Bypass was continually disrupted by protestors.

The metropolis greeted the coming of the automobile with a mixture of open arms and open hostility. New York, like most major American cities, was swiftly choked by traffic, although its island location exacerbated the problem. As the transport historian Clay McShane notes, 'it seems safe to generalize that in the pre-automotive era, large numbers of horses were necessary to move freight within cities; that the size of these herds increased rapidly; and that they posed great problems of cost, pollution and traffic congestion.' McShane points out that by the 1880s, New York was removing up to 15,000 horse carcasses from its streets a year, as well as paying a heavy price in horse-related pedestrian fatalities. New technology provided a solution – first the steamer (a steam-driven carriage which brought its own perils in the form of boiler explosions) and subsequently the internal combustion engine, each hailed as revolutionary aids to city organisation. The automotive future would be free from the dangers and inconvenience of horse- and steam-power, and able to transcend the inflexible iron path of the railways.

Car ownership in America started in cities – due mainly to the wealth of their inhabitants and the better quality of urban roads – and at the turn of the century, New York dominated the American market. The unfortunate New Yorker H.H.Bliss has the unenviable reputation as the first American to be killed by the car on 13 September 1899. Over 3 million have since followed. The first seeds of doubt were sown; the car would be as lethal as the horse, if not more so. Technology has a way of dampening our ardour with its unpleasant side effects. Initially, car-centric planners were undaunted; straighter roads would save lives, bottlenecks were death-traps, pedestrians should vacate the street or face the consequences.

At first, it was envisaged that cities be re-shaped for the benefit of the car and to maintain the social status quo. Middle-class architects were natural allies of the car – owning classes. 'Most architects who did grand city plans shared the motorists' values', notes McShane, cattily yet perceptively, citing Daniel Burnham, the leader of the City Beautiful movement (and also a profound influence on the young Frank Lloyd Wright). 'Clearly [Burnham] and other architects viewed the city mostly as a race track and geometric fantasy for car owners, not a pedestrian-friendly environment.' In addition, City Beautiful plans were vastly expensive, calling for swathes of demolition, and invariably they remained unbuilt, while schemes that did materialise swiftly clogged with traffic. Street widening did little to improve flow, as parked cars consumed the added width.

Mass production and modernisation spawned exponential growth. While the early visionary architectural schemes were aimed at encouraging private car ownership, they were soon struggling to accommodate it. Even the most visionary modernist scheme was not without its glaring flaws. Corbusier's Plan Voisin, aside from being an economic and technical impossibility, would have dominated Paris. In the late 1980s, the scheme was rendered into three dimensions by the shiny computer graphics of the era for a film on the architect's life. The gleaming white towers stood starkly against the jagged skyline of the old town – small wonder that the other motor manufacturers that sponsored the scheme refused to lend their names to it. Kenneth Frampton was moved to note that 'except for the need to gain access to cars parked on the median strip [of the proposed city], there would have been little cause for pedestrians to venture forth into the open.' Corb failed to create a convincing

Bypass
Which came first, the heart bypass, or the town version? Either way, the word symbolises an acute failure of circulation in the organ it is designed to circumvent. But while wealthy cholesterolites are racing to spend their savings on heart surgery, town bypasses have been the subject of some of the most vociferous protests of the late 20th century. The Third Battle of Newbury, as Britain's most famous anti-road showdown became

known, made media stars out of tunnel-digging, tree-dwelling protestors like Swampy, Animal and Muppet Dave in 1996. Despite strong opposition and two public enquiries, plans for the road had been approved. In the end, the best efforts of environmentalists and concerned locals had little impact on the construction of the A34 bypass (apart from adding £25 million to the project's budget to police the site). Four years after building work started, the road was

finally opened to vehicles in November 1998, the momentous occasion marked by a secret late-night ceremony. Less than a year later, the notorious stretch of tarmac was branded a failure: a report by West Berkshire council showed that the bypass had not solved Newbury's congestion problems, and further measures would be necessary. In addition, the road was condemned as being excessively noisy and required resurfacing. While, on this

particular occasion, the road protestors may not have fulfilled their aim of saving a designated area of outstanding natural beauty, three sites of special scientific interest and the scene of a major civil war battle from the bulldozers, they did succeed in turning the humble bypass into a major political issue. Today, new schemes are looming in Salisbury and Hastings, threatening ancient water meadows and the South Downs respectively. Fresh battles beckon.

concrete expression of his famous dictum that the house be a machine for living in, although the Citrohan House of 1921 was to be a 'house like a motor-car, conceived and carried out like an omnibus or a ship's cabin.' Serial production was never achieved. Mass transport spawned strange responses; Wright and Corbusier both studied the possibility of small city cars (and occasionally helicopters) that proved as technically impractical as some of their buildings.

Perhaps most tragically, the concrete reality of Brasília was modernism's most ignominious failure. The project's optimism was dashed by social reality, as the absence of working class housing led to a proliferation of slums. Interaction between the pedestrian and automobile was discouraged, effectively preventing motorists from engaging in activities like shopping and increasing the sense of social alienation between traffic and people. Architectural historian Valerie Fraser believes that, like the Voisin Plan, Brasília's design was informed by its architect's status as a visitor, someone who believed the city should present itself at once as a coherent, understandable whole. One could go further, and argue that to approach the city with the automobile created a skewed set of priorities; just as Voisin's epic towers presented themselves alongside a fast-moving highway, with no immediate means of interaction, Brasília's winged suburbs provided a symbolic, not a practical, solution. The automotive city was damned from the start by its car-centric view, a view which precluded integration from the outset.

When did the carchitecture of popular opprobrium come into existence? Arguably, the architecture of the car has different connotations on each side of the Atlantic. Contemporary American objections to carchitecture focus on suburban sprawl, the miles and miles of retail outlets, fast food joints, drive-thru architecture and parking lots that spread out like bruises between America's cities, creating one long line of shallow, identikit low density, no-place architecture. Historians and theorists of urbanism and transport use the word 'carchitecture', along with 'carburbia' and 'drive-by architecture', to describe this willing submission to the cult of the car.

In just three decades, America's sprawl took on gargantuan proportions, as cities spilled out of their traditional boundaries. The environment of the automobile lost its heroic association and descended into an unwelcoming world of fumes, danger and distance. The long term projections displayed at Futurama might have materialised, yet still they failed to make us happy. Bel Geddes' automotive-powered future of freedom was translated into a latticework of asphalt bars, impounding America behind the all-powerful road lobby, fuel lobby and motor manufacturers, trapping its population a drive, however short, away from where they wanted to get to. Futurism is a fickle profession.

In Britain, carchitecture isn't just sprawl. On a compact, cramped island, it also means the infrastructure of the roads themselves, the slip roads, off-ramps, bridges, bypasses and flyovers that gouge their way so visibly through the environment. Those of us that find beauty and assurance in the uncompromising structure and engineering audacity of these buildings are in a minority. Indeed, only now are the guardians of the nation's heritage slowly accommodating the recent built environment of carchitecture, listing motorway bridges and campaigning against the demolition of car parks. For most people, the road system has descended into

Built as a spur to a multi-storey car-park that never materialised, the infamous 'road to nowhere' in Salisbury adjoined the short stretch of city centre dual carriageway. A popular local landmark and symbol of bureaucratic confusion, it was eventually demolished in the late 1980s. A car park was subsequently built.

**Lay-by**
The status of the lay-by has changed as rapidly as that of the trunk road. Once the symbol of progress, a favourite of forward-thinking planners with an eye for speedy urban regeneration, today the trunk road is the developmental equivalent of the valve amplifier. And the lay-by has followed suit. Back in the days of sideburns and Ted Heath, the lay-by was the perfect spot for a picnic: just pull the Rover out of the traffic, get the hamper out of the caravan, and open a flask of tea. But somewhere along the line, when every lay-by's mobile tea shop had turned into a chip van, and after former England football hero Kevin Keegan was mysteriously assaulted in one while taking a nap in his car, the lay-by became a no-man's-land. Nobody stops in a lay-by any more, except to take a surreptitious pee in the bushes. Dishevelled caravans promising fast food and cold drinks, lorry drivers sleeping in the cabs of their HGVs, or people trying to sell wilting bunches of cheap flowers to long-distance commuters – these are the inhabitants of the lay-by. Full of the driftwood of carchitecture, old rubber tyres and condoms, broken glass and used nappies, it's best to ingore the signs and head for the next Welcome Break service station. Stay on the road.

Opposite above: Designed by Adie Button and Partners with Thomas Bilbow and engineered by A.E.Beer, Stockwell Bus Garage was built on a former bombsite in 1954. Its soaring concrete arches offer the passing motorist an inspirational glimpse into a modernist space devoted to the automotive age. The reinforced beams span nearly 60 metres, dwarfing the double deckers contained within. Opposite below: In the 1971 movie *Get Carter*, Jack Carter (Michael Caine) races down the ramps of Gateshead's Trinity Square

car park in his Sunbeam Alpine, having just grilled a shady character in the building's top floor restaurant (which never opened to the public). The building was designed by Owen Luder and Partners in the mid 1960s in the practice's characteristically brutal style. The car park is currently scheduled for demolition. 'Never mind *Get Carter*, it can get lost,' were the poignant words of a local councillor. Below: A ribbon of concrete: structural engineer Michael Hadi's drawing of an unravelled car park.

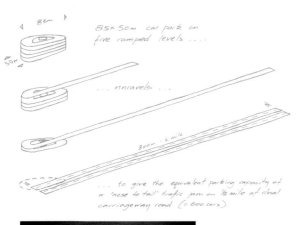

a grey morass. The new motorways, once held with such reverence, couldn't hold their lustre for ever. It wasn't long before the M1's unlimited speed limit was revoked, and the 70 mph national limit introduced (in any case, 70mph had proved too fast for the majority of the nation's cars, as they wheezed up and down the four lanes, expiring messily on the hard shoulder).

Roads had opened up the world. Driving was a pleasurable, not disagreeable activity. Whole cultures thrived around the car – sports, vacations, maintenance, modification – each sustaining and confirming the car's pivotal role at the centre of society. But this popularity wasn't self-sustaining:

'There is a continual tension between the sense of freedom the motorcar brings its owners, and the sense of grievance that crowded roads bring against other car drivers who are seen as limiting that freedom.'
Deyan Sudjic, *The 100 Mile City*, (1992)

Contemporary planning movements are still trying to accommodate this paradox; freedom versus the suffocating crawl this freedom traffic generates. Today, 30% of the average American city is under tarmac; parking lots, garages, streets, flyovers, underpasses, lay-bys. In total, 2% of America is asphalted over, and the drive for open space continues. Housing developments have always been overwhelmingly privately funded, creating suburbs far from the reach of state-subsidised public transport. Size also matters: the American house has increased in size by 40% in the last 25 years, a spread facilitated by widely spaced plots, an almost complete absence of semi-detached properties and a desire for personal, private space. While developer William Levitt didn't perfect the car-led suburb, Levittown, his Long Island development that gently curved across virgin farmland, has become an iconic symbol of the genre. Moving out of the city was now affordable. Today, the average daily commute in America is around 22 miles each way, with Atlanta laying claim to the longest – a 35 mile journey that sees 3 million cars travel 185 million km every day around the city.

America's much-vaunted New Urbanism movement positions itself as 'a reaction to sprawl', creating relatively high-density community-centric developments that strive to undo the dominance of automotive circulation. New Urbanism exists against America's bi-polar attitude to the car – an automotive nation in denial of its own addiction, even when the symptoms are so clearly manifested. Spearheaded by architects Andres Duany and Elizabeth Plater-Zyberk, New Urbanism's aims are set out in their polemical book, Suburban Nation. Duany and Plater-Zyberk propose that America's increasing dependence on the car has alienated large chunks of the population, and suggest that a return to denser, community-centred neighbourhoods will overcome a key reason for submitting to the will of the car – fear of crime. In striving to undo nearly a century of car-driven culture, New Urbanism's thirteen points include the requirement for a defined community centre, with housing located within a five minute walk.

The icon of New Urbanism is Seaside, a retro-styled Florida community built using strict zoning and style laws in an attempt to impose a harmonious environment. Billing itself as 'The Little Beach Town that Changed the World ... By Remembering How Nice the World Can Be', Seaside's main claim to fame is that it was the principal

### Car Park

Once the pride of every bombed out city space, the British car park is in rapid decline. Thanks to the Labour government's commitment to building on brownfield (inner city) sites, and to the awesome rise in urban property prices, car parks are no longer the best way to a quick buck from a patch of land: the real money is in homebuilding. In the 1950s, when concrete was a symbol of progress, multi-storey car parks were *de rigueur* for small towns; a

clear sign that the shoppers were welcome to drive right in. Some represented moments of genuine architectural innovation, like Bertrand Goldberg Associates' Marina City complex in Chicago: the first eighteen storeys of the distinctive 'corn on the cob' apartment towers are given over to clearly visible parked cars. Others, such as Owen Luder's multi-storey in Gateshead, while loved by fans of brutalism, are only celebrated by the wider public because they make

great film sets. The car park has been the subject of considerable architectural research, with at least eight circulation typologies to choose from. Sadly, distinguished new multi-storey car parks have become a rarity. Today, the grim flatlands of the edge-of-town park-and-ride car park, with acres of tarmac veiling the countryside in deep grey, have become the favoured option. Even worse are the undistinguished cages appearing at major airports. Car parks are being

driven underground, hiding beneath city-squares and luxury housing developments alike. Nevertheless, one of Britain's more promising young architectural practices, Birds Portchmouth Russum, began its career with the construction of a multi-storey car park in Chichester in 1991. Rem Koolhaas' Kunsthal in Rotterdam also owes a debt to the design of car parks, with its ramps used to ensure good pedestrian circulation, There's life in the multi-storey yet.

BRASÍLIA
TOMOKO
YONEDA

POLÍCIA MILITAR

POLÍCIA CIVIL

AMBULÂNCIA

CORPO DE BOMBEIROS

location for *The Truman Show* (1998). Peter Weir's anti-media satire seamlessly cast the pastel coloured faux-clapboard houses and candy-floss civic centre as Seahaven, a town which is actually a vast film set, riddled with thousands of cameras and populated with grinning actors conducting an eerily perfect facsimile of day-to-day life. This is anti-carchitecture; the brashness of the freeway or the parking garage has no place in this artificial environment. 'It's okay to misplace your car keys while you're in town,' chirps Seaside's website, 'Strolling is the preferred method of transportation.'

Seaside's 80 acres have proved a tremendous success. Can this small-scale experiment be duplicated? Just a few miles down the Florida coast is Seaside's steroidal big brother, the real-life Seahaven. Celebration is New Urbanism writ large: funded by the might of the Walt Disney Corporation, its bloated 10,000 acre site compares unfavourably to Seaside's compact streets. Celebration will eventually provide for 20,000 residents in a heavily controlled urban environment. Allegedly, Celebration's 'town rules', enforced by roving neighbourhood patrols, stipulate that all window frames must be white or off-white, noisy pets can be evicted and that not more than two people can share a bedroom. Empowering calls to pedestrians are notably absent; Celebration might mimic the little village aesthetic but it is impossible to navigate without a car. 50% of Americans have more than one car, yet another fifth have three. 91% of American households are car-owning – small wonder that New Urbanism must strive to accommodate through concealment, rather than change. Houses at Celebration frequently have large garages .

Ultimately, New Urbanism fails. By choosing as its 'urban' model a form of glossy, romanticised nineteenth century architecture, New Urbanism produces a pre-industrialised, craft-based aesthetic that is both incompatible with contemporary building practices, and with contemporary ways of life. At their worst, New Urbanist schemes aren't about mitigating the effect of the car, but about denying its very existence. Those who buy into the charmed life(style) offered at Seaside and Celebration are choosing to determinedly ignore the problems endemic in their era, just because they can.

Britain's anti-carchitecture movement is spearheaded by Poundbury, a satellite suburb of the Dorset town of Dorchester. Poundbury has received a good deal of attention, most of it stemming from its association with the Prince of Wales, and his much-vaunted (and criticised) architectural views. Poundbury is ostensibly a reaction against the rural and suburban archetype of the cul-de-sac, housing dominated by the garage and driveway, serving only to cut off communities (which are increasingly 'gated') as well as enlarge plot sizes and city sprawl. Yet it is also anti-urban, retrogressive in appearance and mistily idealistic about a rural way of life. In striving to remove the automotive clutter along the ersatz village streets – which come in a variety pack of vernacular-style housing – Poundbury's architects placed the majority of garaging and parking at the rear of the houses. Perhaps unsurprisingly, with so many aspects of life still geared to the car – shopping, school transport, etc. – Poundbury's main streets are now barely used, as people chose to approach their properties from the rear.

Opinion is still sharply divided as to the merits of suburbs. Subtopia, a term coined by the *Architectural Review* in the mid 1950s, is, like carchitecture, ambiguous.

Car Crash
Trust J.G.Ballard to have the nerve to suggest that car crashes have erotic overtones. But in doing so, Ballard breaks one of the car age's curious taboos: the fact is, we can't resist taking a look at the gruesome evidence as we go by. Most people are now aware that traffic congestion is very often caused by motorists slowing down to get a better view of the mangled wreckage, this doesn't prevent us from also trying to sneak a quick peek. Was he really crying? Did you see the way his leg was twisted? Was he dead? Now that it is no longer possible to witness public executions, the car crash is the nearest most of us come to seeing other humans die. At the same time, car safety has represented one of the areas of in-car technology that has seen the greatest advances over the past 20 years, with manufacturers spending vast sums on research and development. In addition to headrests and compulsory seatbelts, we now have driver and passenger airbags in most cars, and specially-designed seats are available for young children. The next generation of cars will go even further, with side airbags, side impact protection, crumple zones, stronger roll bars, and any number of other proprietary gizmos to help prevent you from becoming the next roadside circus act. Thankfully, for car manufacturers it is not car crashes but car safety that is the sexiest issue of our times.

Although suburban living remains aspirational, it's still a yearning for a non-place, an existence between the twin symbols of nationhood; the city and the country. The suburbs exert a fascination, whether it's the grimy windows and soot-stained curtains of the houses along London's Great Western Road, as investigated by Edward Platt in *Leadville*, or the behind-the-net curtain approach adopted by Miranda Sawyer in *Park and Ride*, an exploration of the truth behind the clichéd image of British suburbia. 'Even my car loves the Westway – and on the Westway I love my car,' confesses Platt, as he explores the shattered communities and controversial history of London's Great Western Road. As Platt's book progresses against a backdrop of changing transport policy, *Leadville* becomes a thoughtful paean to the ultimate futility of road-building. Roads are like sponges, he observes – they simply soak up traffic to their maximum capacity. Suburbanisation is torn between two schools of thought. Dismissed by some as the blighted offspring of the city's desire to spread, others – the New Urbanists – see their potential for a return to harmony, order and community. In America, politicians curtail car travel at their peril. In a nation where the bumper sticker is still the prime platform for critical comment, it's unsurprising that the anti-car movement is sidelined.

While the suburbs might appear to be the obvious manifestation of carchitecture – encouraged and nurtured by the extended reach of the internal combustion engine and then condemned to endless motorisation by their spread and lack of centre – there have been concerted attempts to integrate cars and housing in the centre of the city. The Barbican, the central London development that simultaneously acts as a symbol of brutalist excess and a highly successful high-rise, is a good case in point. The Barbican might borrow the brutal aesthetic of the highway engineer, yet it renders it into dynamic domesticity. The key to the centre's success is the integration between car and pedestrian. Admittedly, this actually takes the form of strict segregation – and the Barbican's pedestrian navigation is famously obtuse – but the below decks accommodation for residents and visitors' cars allows a large public space, encompassing such forgotten signs of urbanism as fountains, vantage points and outdoor seating that is actually used. The importance of the car is by no means denied, and perhaps it is the scheme's long gestation (originally proposed in 1959, the Barbican wasn't officially completed until 1979) that has allowed the automobile to slot in so convincingly. Whereas the early modernist schemes were ostensibly pro-car (their dynamic verticality in strict opposition to the suburban sprawl that accompanied the car), little if no provision was made to accommodate the car into their brave new hi-rise world. Occupants of these slabs and towers now look down on the haphazard arrangement of cars which litter their bases, gobbling up the precious landscape their building was designed to preserve.

There was another, more important, impact of these technological developments; the introduction of powered transport totally removed the street's non-travel functions. These roles, the most crucial of which was as a space for social circulation, were lost for ever. The street was no longer an extension of the house or workplace, a place to hang washing, socialise, observe and play. As urban populations adjusted to the faster speed of travel, legislators slowly reduced the oppressive anti-car measures and instead placed the onus on pedestrians to modify their behaviour instead. With changes in transport patterns came a change in the perception of the city, of public space, of the car itself. In America at least, the class differences engendered by the initially expensive technology were transcended by differences of gender and race; the harassment of black motorists began almost as soon as they started driving, while the perceived liberation afforded women drivers threatened masculine roles. Just as today, cars and car use reflected social divides, injustices and intolerance.

Will suburbs continue to bloom for ever? According to a *New York Times* census, American sprawl is slowing – the 1990s saw the suburban population increase by 15%, as opposed to 21% in the 1980s. In Britain, the bucolic aesthetic feels ever-threatened by road building. Rural Britain is central to the country's self-image and it's no surprise that the UK has the most organised and militant anti-roads movement in the world; the nation's small size and diminishing countryside immediately bring the need for new schemes into question. The now legendary stand-offs between protestors and road-builders at Newbury, Bath and Twyford Down were defining national moments, complete with their very own folk heroes. New battles are promised, despite the 1997 Labour government's initial reluctance to follow the Conservative administration's obsession with roads (stemming from Margaret Thatcher's belief in a 'great car economy').

British road protestors can point to countless examples of the cultural and civic vandalism spawned by roads. Car-centric town-planning has produced some of the most desolate and unwelcome cityscapes in the world, not to mention the wanton destruction of irreplaceable built heritage, often needlessly and always regrettably. Many British towns have their monument to misplaced official optimism, in the form of roads to nowhere – sorry-looking flyovers that terminate in thin air as finances and enthusiasm evaporated (in Salisbury, London, Glasgow and many other cities) – to great swathes of housing and shops that became surplus to requirements thanks to the encroaching demands of the car. Tracts of derelict, half-demolished housing along London's A40 bear testament to the abandoned plans for a road-widening scheme, while Claremont Road in East London briefly enjoyed national notoriety as bailiffs sought to replace a squatting community with more lanes of the M11. The bailiffs, inevitably, succeeded.

Road-building is ongoing, never-ending. Cones hotlines contest to our constant awareness of roadworks, potholes, maintenance and the prevalence of luminous orange. We are suffering from an addiction. Town and country is fed by these mechanised drugs plugged into the arterial roads, keeping the system alive. Reyner Banham, wild-eyed and strung-out from the speeding exhilaration of Los Angeles's free-for-all freeways, summed it up by saying 'the freeway system in its totality is now a single comprehensible place, a coherent state of mind, a complete way of life, the fourth ecology of the Angeleno... The freeway is where the Angelenos live a large part of their lives.' When Banham composed his ode to Los Angeles, using the car to tour the city's architectural delights, he noted that LA's freeways 'worked remarkably well.' Thirty years have proved unkind to his enthusiasm, and even grandiose engineering schemes like the Century Freeway, an eight-lane, 27 km, $3 billion stretch of road, have failed to alleviate LA's choking traffic. Today, over 5 million Angelenos commute via car. Three quarters of a million take public transport.

London's concession to urban autopianism is the Westway, a far cry from the flying

**Speed hump**
The 'sleeping policeman' is, in fact, dead. Over the past decade, driving has been invaded by a new and altogether more prolific traffic-calming menace: the speed hump. Otherwise known as vertical deflectors, road humps, speed cushions or speed tables, these scourges of the urban environment have probably had more influence on taking the joy out of motoring than anything else. What's worse, many people living near a speed hump have found that the noise created as cars slow down and then accelerate away is every bit as annoying as the higher traffic speed prior to their introduction. Recent improvements to the design of speed humps have meant that emergency vehicles can usually now straddle them without causing fatal damage to passengers with spinal injuries en route to hospital (they still inflict maximum discomfort on the average motorist, of course). But the single biggest problem caused by the invasion of speed humps has been the diversion of traffic onto other nearby roads, often leading to even greater congestion on arterial routes. To date, there is no evidence that vertical deflectors have led to any reduction in fatal road accidents in London. Just a bonanza for the manufacturers of shock absorbers.

eight-laners that criss-cross LA. It was not a popular development. In 1969, J. Michael Thomson wrote in *Motorways in London* that the city has 'coped with motor traffic for over half a century without motorways and will have to cope with the motorways for a very long time if they are built... It is better to spend more time looking for a way out of the quagmire than to risk plunging further in.' The Westway is the surviving relic of a transport policy that held the car in indecent respect – respect for the motor industry, at the time a major source of revenue – and for the inalienable rights of the car-owning, voting public. Yet the road is undeniably impressive. Soaring high above west London, it continues to enthral artists, architects and writers, with its unparalleled urban views. J.G.Ballard's *Crash* (1973) told of the 'solid reality of the motorway embankments, with their constant and unswerving geometry', yet these are now clichéd symbols of edgy urban appreciation.

Roads beget roads. Clearly, we haven't stopped using our cars. Those quick to damn the picture-postcard banality of our built environment –the carchitecture of popular legend, why-oh-why columns and *That's Life* style 'boring postcards' – are most likely car owners themselves. Carchitecture's opponents continue to champion the car – often the most technologically advanced consumer item they will ever own, with R&D costs running into the billions. Ironically, they house these miracles of mass production within an aesthetic that seeks to nip and tuck at modernism's more excessive moments, shaping their automotive experience into something altogether more genteel. Think of the mock-Tudor garage, for example. For many, the no-storey car park – a sea of undulating tarmac surfed by a muddy foam of sunroofs and steel – is preferable to the blunt vulgarity of the concrete garage, with its explicit purpose and modernist origins. Instead, the multi-storey is subject to a raft of indignations – concealed, buried, façaded – a pariah in the cityscape. Urbanism, and by association, modernity, is still something the car helps us escape.

'The S40 1.8 Sport is the perfect antidote to the rigours of urban life. Its air conditioned, woven/leather upholstery and sophisticated CD system keeps you relaxed and stress free. Its world-leading safety and security features offer reassuring levels of protection. And when you escape the city streets to the open road, the responsive 122 bhp engine delivers an exhilarating driving experience.' Advertisement for Volvo, (2001)

As the car evolved, becoming sleeker and more agile, the antagonism between ancient and modern, motion and stasis, increased, with stasis – architecture – conceding defeat. It was architecture which bent before the car, straightening curves, dipping and bending, letting the car run riot around the foot of our buildings. Architecture reared up and ceased to address the street. New York cut down the trees that lined its new boulevards – they obstructed motorists' vision and impaired their safety. The architect and writer Michael Sorkin believes that our city life can be described in terms of traffic. 'Modern culture,' he observed, 'is increasingly characterized by suspension in capsules of intermediacy: in trains, planes, automobiles and elevators, not to mention time spent on-line with electronic styles of mobility.'

Sorkin notes that while ceaseless traffic flow is carchitecture's aim – efficiency made visible – this emphasis on constant movement denies the equally important

**Road rage**
From Los Angeles to Glasgow, London to Delhi, road rage is the crime of our age. Pedestrians, passengers, dogs and racehorses have all fallen victim to the blind fury of a driver or passer-by scorned in an encounter with a car. Where once car-jacking and traffic light Rolex-snatchers were the number one worry for the anxious urban motorist, road rage now has the edge. London's recent litany of horrors included a kneecapping,

while Americans spent the summer hooked on the unfolding saga of Andrew Burnett, accused of hurling fluffy Leo into oncoming traffic after an altercation with the dog's owner. Irate Americans, snapped out of their reverie by this most heinous of crimes, contributed over $100,000 reward to catch the dog's killer. Most road rage crimes are far less sensational, their tawdry, unprovoked drama evoking only disbelief and pity. The randomness of road rage threatens to destabilise

our automotive isolation; when every other motorist or pedestrian is a threat to your life, it's best to drive defensively and keep the doors locked. Claw hammers, knives, guns and fists - even the car is used as a weapon. Congestion certainly shoulders some of the blame; in America, traffic has increased by 35% in 15 years, yet there are only 1% more roads. Statistics suggest that incidents of 'violent aggressive driving' are increasing by 7%, year on year. Of

course, antagonism between cars, drivers and pedestrians has always existed, it just took the snappy term 'road rage' to bring it onto the front pages. Advice? Thus far, official bodies in America have offered only the following pronouncements – 'avoid eye contact – Making eye contact with an aggressive driver usually leads to an exacerbated situation.' And finally: 'Accept traffic – while traffic is inconvenient, accept it because it is currently a permanent part of life.'

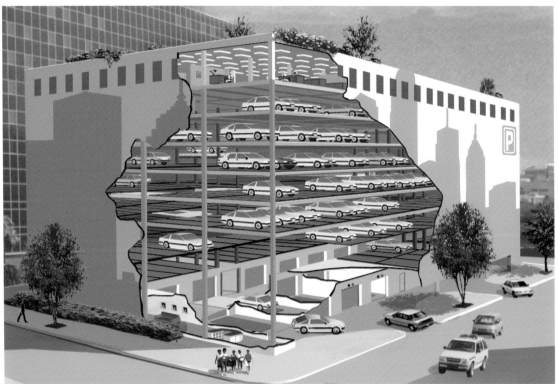

# A MACHINE FOR PARKING IN

ALEX STETTER

In the world's biggest, busiest cities, there simply aren't enough parking spaces to go round. The frustration of being stuck in a permanent urban traffic jam is compounded by the knowledge that on finally reaching your destination, you will still have to find somewhere semi-legal to abandon your vehicle. In fact, it's more than likely that half the cars around you don't qualify as proper through-traffic at all, they're just fellow would-be parkers, on their fifth circuit of the neighbourhood.

The logical conclusion is to make maximum use of the small amount of free space available by going upwards. But high-rise car parks have an image problem; people tend to think of them as concrete eyesores with smelly stairwells, if they think of them at all.

Companies like Robotic Parking, Inc. in Ohio believe the answer lies in total automation: machines for parking in. Mechanical garages first appeared in the US in the 1930s, but were destined to remain a curiosity

at a time when space was hardly at a premium. For a brief period in the 1970s and 1980s, the idea enjoyed limited popularity in the less space-rich cities of Asia and Europe.

RoboPark have updated the basic concept by introducing transport technology developed for car assembly lines to make the process as swift and smooth as possible. You drive into an entry bay the size of a single garage, get out, take a ticket and stand well clear while your vehicle is whisked away into the

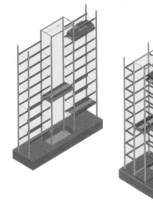

heart of the building-cum-machine. On your return, the parking robot takes just two minutes to retrieve your car. With no valuable parking space taken up by ramps or pedestrian walkways and no need for ventilation or lighting, this type of structure is very cost effective, making room for twice as many cars as usual by cutting out the human element completely.

RoboPark pride themselves on their product's flexibility. Their modular parking system can be extended, relocated, made to fit into any structure and clad in any finish. But while these would all be highly desirable attributes to find in a flat-pack bookshelf, they do not necessarily make for a good building, one that engages with and enhances its environment.

Hidden behind an anonymous exterior, the car park's function is denied and not expressed, let alone celebrated. It's the perfect response to our automotive guilt: making robots deal with our cars, out of sight to keep our consciences clear.

role of the destination, or node. Observing that 'nodal architectures subsumed by strategies of flow are predominant in the American landscape: the strip, the shopping mall, the suburbs, the edge city, everything,' Sorkin cites the failed attempts of planners and architects to facilitate the interaction of pedestrians and traffic. Traffic inevitably dominates. Not only does traffic subjugate its environment, it subjugates itself. The word 'Gridlock' was coined by traffic engineers in New York in the 1970s, some sixty years after the traffic jam was 'invented'. Studies reveal that at any given moment, just 9,000 cars are in motion in New York; the rest are frozen, in a moment of stasis, patiently (or not so patiently) awaiting their turn to inch closer to their destination.

Writer and theorist Jane Holtz Kay suggests in her book *Asphalt Nation: How the Automobile Took Over America and How We Can Take It Back* (1998), that carchitecture is the sprawl of concrete and tarmac that starts at the off-ramp, rarely stops and ensures cities are forever slaves to the automobile. The fundamental flaw in interstate planning still resonates through American society. While small communities sprang up alongside the routes in rural areas, interstates either skirted major towns or plunged straight through the suburbs, dividing whole neighbourhoods and forming the basis for community divisions. The 'other side of the tracks' became the other side of the road. Yet others see carchitecture simply as a manifestation of the city's ability – and willingness – to change and accommodate. Some cities, like Boston, even embrace the term, albeit warily, in planning documents that describe the ever-increasing emphasis architecture places on accommodating the car. With 600,000 commuters cars entering Boston each day, the city embarked on an old-fashioned attempt to solve the problems of urban congestion with vast investments in infrastructure. The elevated highway carried over twice as much traffic as envisaged when it opened in 1959, creating traffic jams that lasted 'eight to ten hours a day', predicted to rise to 16 hours a day by 2010.

Boston's solution is the Central Artery/Tunnel, the 'Big Dig', billed as the 'largest, most complex and technologically challenging engineering project in American history.' The 12 km corridor through the centre of the city will be augmented with 161 new traffic lanes, threaded above, through and under each other, over half of which are underground, in an attempt to channel daily loads of up to a quarter of a million vehicles. The Big Dig is, perhaps surprisingly, billed as an environmental improvement. The primary focus is a new park above the buried road, a linear green space that will sit atop the expanded highway, banishing it from view. Spoil – some 3 million cubic yards – from the works are being used to transform a former municipal dump into an 105 acre park at Spectacle Island.

Even roads' association with economic prosperity is under fire. Environmental audits suggest that American motorists should be paying approximately $5 a gallon in order to compensate for the damage cars do to their surroundings. Of course, such a price would be unworkable in the current – and foreseeable future – American political climate. Petrol currently costs approximately $1.50 a gallon, of which just over 50% is tax (compared to 75% in the UK). With gas at the lowest price for 75 years and an oil man in the White House, there is little incentive to improve fuel consumption. *Harper's* magazine recently calculated that the daily US petrol consumption would drop by nearly 50,000,000 gallons if SUVs (Sports Utility

Opposite: London's Mile End Millennium Park, designed by Piers Gough of CZWG, represents a bold reclamation of the urban environment. The 29 hectare park contains a five-lane wide structure – the Green Bridge – spanning 25 metres across the Mile End Road to 'mend' two sections of the divided park. The architecture of transport no longer dominates nature instead, it helps it regain its place in the city.

### Cones Hotline

One of the best known – some would say only – acts of John Major's doomed Conservative administration was the creation of the notorious Cones Hotline in 1992. As part of the Prime Minister's much-vaunted 'Citizen's Charter', a freephone number was set up to enable irate British motorists to vent their fury on the chief obstacle of the age: the road cone. The Cones Hotline swiftly descended into farce – a supposedly empowering service, it was derided for its ineffectiveness and as a waste of public money. Major chronically misjudged the motorist's mood – become surrounded by a sea of pointy orange cones and the last available option in the pre-mobile age was to pull over and dial up a government switchboard. The Cones Hotline survived the Conservative's catastrophic disintegration, but only just. After a few months as the subject of numerous mocking questions in Parliament, ably fielded by Glenda Jackson, it eventually faded out of public memory and segued into the equally ineffective Highways Agency Information Line (HAIL). In HAIL's first year of operation, from September 1995 to August 1996, just 319 anxious members of the public called the line with a query about the dreaded conical pieces of plastic. And they're still with us, in their millions. HAIL: 08457 504 030

Vehicles) were just 3 mpg more efficient. A 100kg reduction in weight saves half a litre of fuel every 100 km; little wonder that the SUV has become a prime environmental target.

Today, all road schemes are accompanied by reports, hefty calculations of environmental impact that weigh up pros and cons, for and against, loss versus gain. The truth can no longer be concealed; roads cut through cities, radiating out from them and criss-crossing the countryside, permanently scarring and blighting. Yet it wasn't until the 1970s that environmental considerations began to be incorporated into planning procedure. Well-publicised reports like the Club of Rome's 1972 *The Limits to Growth*, projected a gloomy future, culminating in a doomsday scenario that projected economic and social collapse within a century due to spiralling land use and demand. For the first time, it was acknowledged that natural resources were finite. Today, the world's richest 20% consume 86% of its goods and over 50% of its energy. America, home to 5% of the world's population, creates 25% of the world's $CO_2$ emissions. Holtz Kay cited how cars pollute during production, pointing out that 'before the motor vehicle had even left the plant, the car-to-be had produced 29 tons of waste and 1,207 million cubic yards of polluted air.' *The Limits to Growth* also coincided with the 1973 fuel crisis, a very visible sign of the frailty of the systems that supported western-style car-devotion. Speed limits were cut to 55mph across America, and the 'gas guzzler' era appeared to be over.

By the outbreak of WWII, Ford's River Rouge factory in Detroit covered some 33 square kilometres. Today, the city is a ghost town. The towering Michigan Central Railroad Station stands forlorn and empty in the middle of a wasteland, like a new hotel alone on Las Vegas's arid Strip. Part of Ford's original Highland Park site is now a shopping mall, with jaunty signs proclaiming 'Model T Plaza'. America's car industry consolidated, merged, split and floundered. When it finally recovered, Motorcity was surplus to requirements. Globalisation had finally finished with the motor-car's birthplace.

In recent years, the car industry has torn itself apart. Production is dominated by five companies, GM, Ford, Toyota, VW and DaimlerChrysler, each owning a mass of brands, marques and subsidiaries. GM, which makes about 8 million vehicles a year, consists of 12 brands, from Saab to Cadillac, with manufacturing bases spread from Australia to Sweden, while VW and Ford each have five or more individual brands. Yet globalisation and the multinational's desire to tout around for the production centre with the lowest overheads have seen the car factory transformed into wandering nomad. Despite a European car market of 15 million units a year, production capabilities are vastly higher; Europe's car factories have the capacity to build six million more cars than can be sold. Clearly, someone's betting on a long-term strategy. For now, the industry counters this extra capacity with round after round of mergers and acquisitions, seeking new markets and new, ever cheaper production centres. The ultimate goal is Asia, where low car ownership and high populations are spurring Western companies to invest in plant and marketing. Yet although global car sales – and more crucially profits – are falling, car numbers continue to rise.

Opposition that had been festering for decades came to the fore; carchitecture has enemies in unlikely sources. Film historian David Thomson argues that *Who Framed*

**Traffic wardens**
Nobody likes traffic wardens. No other profession is as liable to be on the receiving end of both verbal and physical abuse from members of the public on a daily basis. No other profession is so certain to pit one human against another in a battle of the individual against the system. Before it dawned on Local Governments that there was serious money to be made from parking offences, we accepted 'Lovely Rita, meter maid' as a necessary control mechanism; a friendly figure who ensured that our streets were kept free of inconsiderately parked cars, as well-respected as the local policeman. But new attitudes to money turned traffic wardens into commission-based vultures with quotas to fill, touring the streets with grim determination. And who can blame them? These teams of patrol-people are busy collecting serious money for their masters. Traffic wardens now collect millions of pounds in parking fines in London, of which a fair portion is reinvested in improving the road system. We may no longer trust them, but traffic wardens are responsible for a significant contribution to the public realm, the absence of which would probably mean urban chaos and substantially increased income tax. Just don't let them anywhere near *my* car.

*Roger Rabbit*, (1988), Robert Zemeckis's Oscar-winning mix of live action and animation, is the concluding part of Robert Towne's projected Los Angeles trilogy, which started with *Chinatown* (1974) and continued, after a 16 year hiatus, with *The Two Jakes*. While the first two films were concerned with the double deals that shadowed LA's inception, the battles for oil and water that shaped the land, *Roger Rabbit's* plot focuses on the freeway. 'Who'll use the freeways,' asks Bob Hoskins' Private Investigator, Eddie Valiant, 'when the city has Red Car trolley buses, the best public transportation in the country?' 'Not for long. We're retiring the Red Cars. People will drive, Mr Valiant, because they'll have to. And when they drive, they'll have to buy our cars, our tires, our gasoline,' replies Christopher Lloyd's sinister Judge Doom. The more conspiratorially-minded can read the black-clad Doom as a thinly caricatured Le Corbusier, complete with thick, round glasses and an obsession with roads.

Driving is a game of give and take, a battle of wits that ultimately leads to our destination; anywhere but the road. The optimism of this age is over. Highways agencies the world over talk technology – nation-wide tracking systems that will alert and divert us, freeing the motorist once more to seek out the open, unencumbered road.

> 'Today... streets serve primarily as storage spaces and racetracks for motor cars that are absolutely incompatible with traditional street functions ... the modern American metropolis is a socially and politically fragmented, gas-guzzling environmental nightmare.' Clay McShane, *Down the Asphalt Path*, (1994)

Even the car's glory days didn't last. Before long, the sheer volume of cars on the roads encouraged the authorities to seek new methods of control. The term 'traffic jam' was coined as early as 1910 and stop signs, traffic lights (1920s), one-way streets and parking restrictions soon followed. These have been joined by parking meters (1958), radar guns (1958), humps, in their modern form dating from the 1970s, speed cameras (1986) and 24-hour parking cameras (2001). In the modern age, these controlling technologies have become integrated into the architecture of our cities, motorways and country lanes, invisibly watching over our automotive behaviour. Popular belief holds that Gatso cameras lie concealed within leafy glades and tucked behind road signs, all the better to eke more revenue from the passing motorist. Britain has more CCTV cameras per head of population than anywhere else on earth; some 1.5 million of them, many trained on our roads and intersections, sitting atop high poles, beaming their imagery to banks of screens in some remote location, occasionally churning out comic moments for our televisual entertainment. Carchitecture is a state of control, an environment monitored and overseen, squeezed by rules and desperate for more space. We're not going back.

Cities, towns, villages and countryside consider the car to be simultaneously friend and foe. For the pessimist, the car's friendly face has long since disappeared, condemning our society to co-exist with a sociopathic menace. Cars beget strange new architecture and environments; only now are we deciding it's a world we're unwilling to share for much longer. To conclude that modernism failed due to its car dependence is unfair. Yet few would disagree that we are now living in an auto dystopia of our own making.

**Traffic calming**
Those who live in country villages tend to be very proud of the beauty of their community. On arriving in an average village, visitors can expect to be welcomed by a sign proclaiming it winner of an award for the *Surrey In Bloom Most Beautiful Public Flower Display, 1983*, or some similarly warm-hearted enterprise. But this passion for civic beauty has, in a near universal change of heart by rural folk, recently been replaced by the new, altogether more zealous pursuit known as traffic calming. It is no secret that cars tend to ignore speed limits in villages, having screeched their way through the rural lanes between them, and so it was no real surprise when the sign for each village in the land suddenly started gaining a subtitle: Please Drive Carefully. But signs proclaiming that *Down Ampney Welcomes Careful Drivers* were just the first symptom of the new traffic calming plague. Now, you can expect to have to negotiate chicanes, cross over a rumble strip, give way to oncoming traffic in a one-lane filter, traverse brightly coloured tarmac and face a barrage of road signs imploring you to slow down. *Kill Your Speed, Not a Child!* It's all very laudable, and almost certainly fatalities have decreased in the process, but the resulting visual cacophony makes every village look like an *It's a Knockout* assault course. And if eye-witness accounts are to believed, the locals themselves are often the worst offenders, guilty of completely ignoring the warnings and thundering along familiar village roads at breakneck speed in the rush to get on with life.

# HARD SHOULDER, SOFT SELL

CLARE DOWDY

The showroom was once a space of novelty, a new building type that soared high above the vehicles on display. Auguste Perret's reinforced concrete Garage Ponthieu in Paris (1906) was a remarkable structure, with vast panels of glass covering the slender façade – the industrial aesthetic applied as a celebration of technology.

Fast forward 95 years, and the brave new world of car retail has segued into a morass of low-level sprawl, off-the-shelf showrooms with zero personality and presence, blossoming out along arterial roads. Only the flagship showroom – the big brand, high-rent billboard sites that line Park Lane and the Champs Elysées – transcend the stereotype. Otherwise, it's bad coffee in Styrofoam cups, an old copy of the *Mirror* to peruse, bland decor, product over-crowding, aggressive staff and an atmosphere that borders on the hostile. This was, until recently, the experience of visitors to British car showrooms. The dealership is the last bastion of retail to be touched by the concepts of customer experience and design, but it is catching up fast. It is now having to redress its complacency, especially as it has become seriously out of step with Europe, where car manufacturers are using the currency of modern architecture, and even the promise of family entertainment, to promote their brands.

Away from the pedestrian world of the car showroom, reliant on passing trade and established sites, there are other architectural structures. A breed apart from the conventional showroom, claiming more grandiose motives than merely flogging motors, these new projects represent the apogee of contemporary commercial carchitecture. These are the buildings which aim to promote a manufacturer's identity, and as a result they are architectural phenomena in their own right.

Perhaps able to trace their origins back to Matté-Trucco's remarkable Fiat factory in Lingotto, Turin, in the 1930s, architecture is harnessed to display not just the vehicles, but the design philosophy and power of the manufacturer. Trucco's factory is best known for its rooftop test track, which represented the end of the production process. Freshly-finished cars were taken for an exploratory lap before twirling down the elegant concrete ramp and out into the marketplace. While in the majority of cases, the physical location has not changed – arterial roads are still crammed with silvery-clad auto dealerships – the new breed of commercial carchitecture is branching out into hitherto unknown territory. VW is making the most blatant attempt to recreate the total environment of Trucco's Lingotto plant through its 'transparent manufactory', a glass-walled factory in Dresden currently under construction. In London's

Opposite: Behind the massive car towers of VW's Autostadt park at Wolfsburg, the factory chimneys are brightly lit. Above: Apart from a service centre for customers picking up their new cars, the site contains a five-star hotel, 360°cinema, restaurants and six pavilions, one for each marque in the VW group (Audi, Bentley, Lamborghini, Skoda, Seat and VW), all set within a landscape of artificial lakes and manicured lawns. Nick Swallow, of designers Furneaux Stewart, who were responsible for the VW and Bentley pavilions, describes the new ventures as 'architecture which pays homage to cars'. BMW are now in on the act, with their Event/Delivery centre in Münich, a palace of automotive consumption by New York practice Asymptote Architects.

Soho, Ford is opening its new Design Centre, with design critic and curator Stephen Bayley at the helm, in a building designed (on spec) by Richard Rogers.

VW Autostadt in Wolfsburg is a vast automotive theme park, complete with five-star hotel, landscaped grounds and a range of car-related attractions, all planned by Volkswagen's favoured project architect Dr Henn. Targeted not only at German customers coming to collect their new cars from the VW works, Autostadt is also promoted as a destination for a family day out. The park's formula and atmosphere will be familiar to anyone who has visited a recent Expo. Key features of the site are the six pavilions devoted to the brands owned by the German manufacturer. Some of the pavilions attempt to act almost as educational facilities, often relying on mini-cinemas to impress the visitor, raising brand awareness while also giving off a benevolent sheen that – VW hopes – will reflect well on its position in the marketplace.

The pavilions are arranged around shallow lakes, surrounded by supplementary attractions such as a skating rink and restaurants – the main building features car-related rides for children. There are surprisingly few actual cars on display in the pavilions: the structure devoted to the VW marque is in the form of a glass cube which contains a large sphere. The inside of this sphere serves as a projection screen for a film showing two young girls learning to play the violin, intended to convey VW's 'constant, step-by-step striving for perfection'. This connection is reinforced on leaving the cinema, when the bemused visitor is confronted with vitrines filled with shiny chromed car innards, presented under museum-style lighting. All this takes place in front of the backdrop of the massive VW factory chimneys, lit at night by huge coloured arc lights,

so that both chimney and plume take on a Disney-like innocence.

So is Autostadt simply a triumph of architecture over content, or a sign of the gradual demise of the traditional showroom? Design practitioners, reared on a diet of glassy street façades, polished cars and potted plants, feel they are pushing back the boundaries of these hackneyed environments. To a certain extent, the new devices they are introducing reflect the industry's desire for diversification, however superficial, focusing on the aspiration created by the brand, and not just the model in hand. Designers' claims that they are trying 'to make the buying experience different' (Mike Booth of Design House, currently working with Toyota), through the creation of 'customer journeys' ties in neatly with the industry's desire to increase their presence in our lives.

Thus the 'brand lobby', a physical space intended to immerse

the customer in the values of the brand, has been vastly scaled up; a wall of Jaguar umbrellas and golf clubs is nothing when compared to the immersive environments of Autostadt, Audi's Museum or Ford's Design Centre.

Multiple, varied zones are becoming commonplace even in the traditional showroom, as mergers bring disparate brands together into one physical space (witness BMW's frantic reorganisation of its showrooms to accommodate the new Mini, allowing the upmarket brand to remain cosseted from its cheaper stablemate).

These new, all-encompassing locations beg more questions than the traditional showroom. Ford's Design Centre, for example, is wilfully misleading – it won't function as a space where the company's draughtsmen will slave over details of next year's models. Instead, the Design Centre promises to be little more than

Opposite and above: Keeping one eye on their future customer base, VW have made sure Autostadt includes plenty of attractions for children, from go-karts to a huge model of a combustion engine with a slide for an exhaust pipe. Right: In December 2000, Audi opened the Museum Mobile, part of the new Audi-Forum at their headquarters in Ingolstadt. Dedicated to the history of the company and the development of the car, the museum takes visitors from the days when people still bought petrol by the canister from a chemist's shop right up to the latest prototypes.

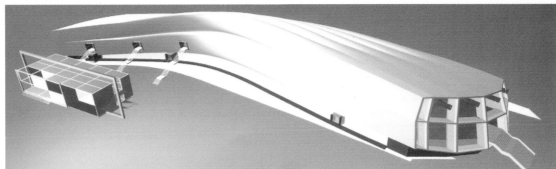

a slick PR exercise, a space where Ford can present design, albeit design filtered through the company's world view.

Autostadt is similarly prescriptive – a family day out that is built on the premise of a car-dependent future. In this respect, it is perhaps the perfect showroom, akin to a form of mass sublimation whereby the message becomes so ubiquitous, it no longer needs a medium. Autostadt's synthesis of lifestyle and product is conveyed through an exaggerated, unrealistic architecture, in which the virtues of product are reduced to undemanding spectacle. Unlike the Dresden factory, there is no explicit acknowledgement of the actual manufacturing process, although the huge VW plant is next door.

Car manufacturers are finding new ways to sell, ways which impact our lives in ever more visible ways. From small-scale brand kiosks, like the two-car BMW showroom and coffee shop, Sytner, in the City of London, to shop-style spaces and environments dedicated to all-important after-care and servicing, to the megastructures of the car-centric theme park, we are promised that the showroom – like cars themselves – will offer us more and more. The new, bolder, bigger showroom edges the automobile deeper into the consumer's consciousness, extending the brand into the psychogeography of our cities, spaces that serve our ever-increasing desire for consumer identity.

Opposite: At a height of 30 metres, this tower designed by German compact parking specialists Wöhr for a Toyota dealership in Gelsenkirchen is the tallest of its type in the country, and has become a local landmark.
Above: The ultimate in car display technology, Saab dealership, Germany.
Top: For the 2001 Frankfurt Motor Show, BMW commissioned the dramatic 130-metre long Dynaform pavilion, designed using the latest imaging software from the film and automotive industries.
Right: Eye-catching glass display towers played a key role in the marketing of the Smart car.

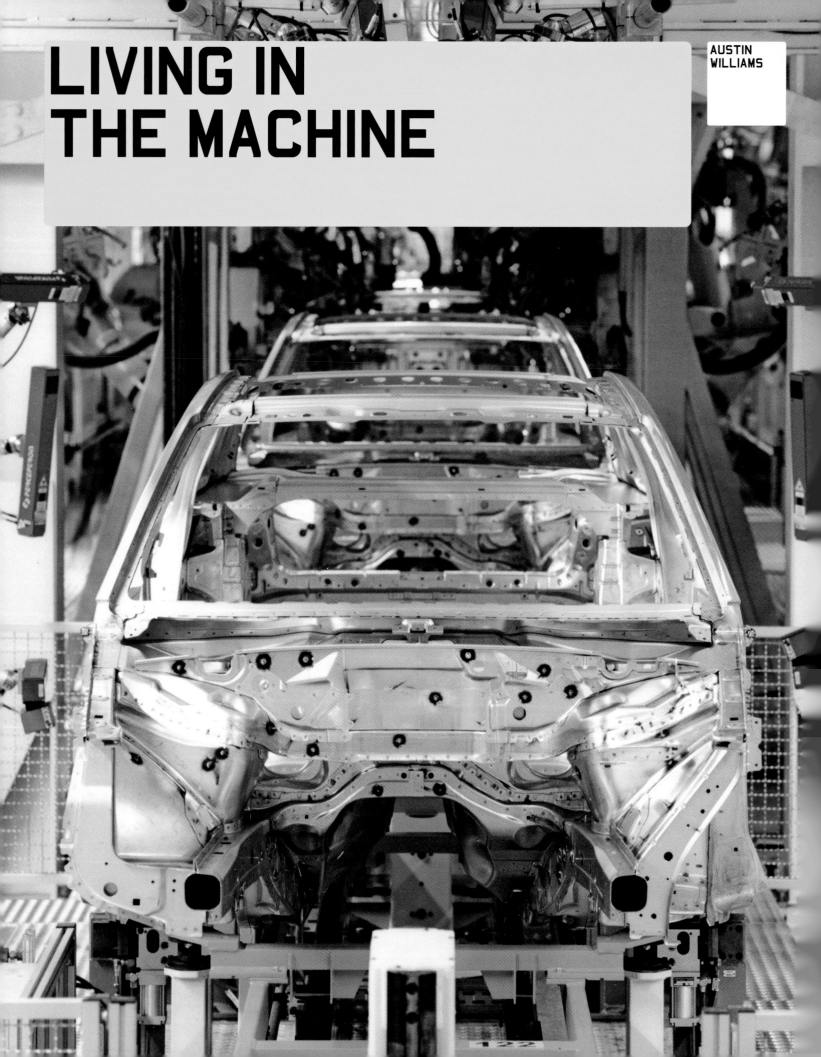

# LIVING IN THE MACHINE

AUSTIN
WILLIAMS

Anybody who has ever been employed in an architect's office, worked on a building site or even simply watched a house being erected, will realise that the process of getting a building built is a fragmented, confused and often wasteful set of operations. Wasteful in labour, time and money.

Recognising that things are in need of tightening up, government and manufacturers have looked to the car industry as an example of how things could be better organised, especially learning from automotive production which 'effortlessly' integrates a wide range of repetitive processes into a co-ordinated whole. Even given the shaky state of worldwide car manufacturing, the industry's accelerated production line processes are impressive in comparison with the linear procedures typical of the 'traditional' construction sector.

However, it is worth remembering that not long ago, the UK car industry was going through a similar crisis. Manufacturing was deemed to be inefficient, labour-intensive and inflexible. The shake-up of traditional working practices was industry-wide. When the so-called Japanese models of lean thinking and Just-in-Time manufacture arrived, the workforce was suitably geared up to accept the more rationalised working environment. A study of Nissan, one of the first Japanese manufacturers to set up in Britain, concluded:

> 'Behind the glossy adverts and the dependable image of the car makers, the world's largest industry is being shaken to its foundations. But in the midst of the Car Wars the world is being taken apart and put together again to suit the needs of the strongest combatants.'

The rationalising of work practices 20 years ago, together with massive levels of investment in the form of set-up loans, tax credit and pump-primed financial dealings, enabled the powerful multinational car market to create a more amenable environment for production line economies. But while robots are commonplace in manufacturing, they do not appear on building sites.

So even though there has been huge government support to the construction industry in the form of grants, lottery projects, Housing Association funding and other hidden subsidies, why haven't highly automated manufacturing processes translated into the construction sector? The obvious answer is that the process of design and construction has evolved into a historically diffuse industry. The UK has an on-site workforce of 1.5 million divided between 10,000 building firms, without taking into account the 25,000 architects and similar numbers of quantity surveyors and mechanical and electrical engineers working in thousands of separate companies, achieving an annual turnover of £65 billion. This compares with 110,000 car workers (not including the 150,000 involved in component and parts manufacture and approximately 20,000 in design) employed by 40 main producers making maybe ten models each, yet turning over £30 billion.

The difference is plain to see. While there are regular attempts at exerting authority over the diverse construction industry – like the current pressure to eliminate 'cowboy' builders from the register of acceptable contractors – no showdown similar to that which occurred in automobile manufacturing in the 1970s and 1980s has taken place with the building sector. In fact, the generalised comparisons between automotive manufacturing and architectural production are difficult to sustain. These are of course very different 'products': one with a life expectancy of 3-5 years, the other a lifetime; one moves, the other remains static; one for travelling, the other for study, play or sleep. Although there have been flights of architectural fancy trying to challenge these paradigms – most notably Archigram and SITE Architects schemes in the 1970s – the functional disparities between the two sectors remain. The public's demands on architecture are culturally attuned to different expectations than those of the single-issue pleasure of their car.

Even though sustainability advocates imply that a home should be for life, homeowners still prefer to customise their dwellings by adding

Opposite: Before the A4 passes on to the next stage of the production line at Audi's Ingolstadt plant, the monocoque structure is checked and measured by lasers, achieving a level of accuracy impossible in the construction industry.

a conservatory or repainting as soon as they move in. The Japanese model of finished 'pods' doesn't seem to connect with the British market sensibility at present. Where inroads have been made into mass production, in housebuilding in particular, local cultural norms seem to determine the limits to its successful implementation. As Raymond Ogden, Professor of Architectural Technology at Oxford Brookes University says: 'Standardisation will be difficult in anything other than components, since different regions want different designs. Even Yorkon or Terrapin, where they are working on mass production units, are doing it at a very small scale.' However, the certainties derived from prefabrication mean that it is no longer viewed with the contempt it once was. Over the years, society has become less tolerant of defective products. Nowadays, we want modern standards of comfort, speed and flexibility. Maybe, as some argue, this heightened expectation has been driven by our experience of cars and their production values. As Alison Smithson observed:

'Our sensibilities have been affected by our use of our "room on wheels" but also, there comes a new awareness of the responsibilities inherent in our comfortable view of just about anywhere. Our idea of quality of place, our will to bring through quality in all things, these should also be affected by our possession of a cell of perfected technology'

The links between the machine-inspired technology of car production and the aspiration to transfer the technology over to architecture is long established (compare what Piers Gough calls 'the relentless logic of the terraced house' to the inter-war Ford plant conveyor belt). Whether implicitly or explicitly, this has affected much of the architectural traditions of the 20th century, from Walter Gropius to Walter Segal. However, even these pioneers realised, from different perspectives, that prefabrication could not produce 'whole-house' delivery, suitable to satisfy the very real individual desires of the house-buying market. Rather, the aim was for standardised components that could be plugged into the mainframe. As far back as 1909, Walter Gropius noted that, 'only the standardisation of component parts could "satisfy the public desire for a home with an individual appearance"'

Currently, the aspects of motor production which are driving the attempts to shake up construction concern Just-in-Time (JIT), or lean, production. This involves buying in only those stocks that are necessary for immediate use, thereby cutting down on storage costs as well as

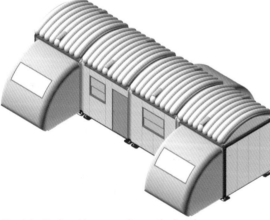

Top right: Designed in 1997 by B Consultants using flat-pack construction components, the 'Rollalong' modular building unit provides an effective temporary solution for offices, schools and hospitals in need of some additional space. Above: Alessandro Laterza's 'Dado System – Provvisorio Flessibile' is an Italian take on the pre-fab housing system. Right: Cartwright Pickard Architects designed an innovative housing scheme for the Peabody Trust at Murray Grove in East London, based on pre-fabricated modules trucked to the site and assembled by crane.

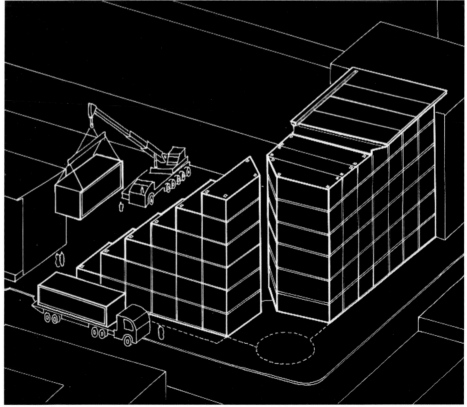

BT's 'plug-in' office module makes effective use of production line technology. Designed by the Building Design Partnership, the project maximises off-site construction. Using ready-made buildings means the office complex can expand easily and quickly.

wastage, and helping cash-flow, with less capital tied up in production. Even though this causes the economic burden to be passed down the supply chain, it is a more efficient means of production which undoubtedly benefits the consumer by leading to lower costs.

Now, demand for better choices within the automotive industry (amongst others) requires that customer choice should be inputted into the mass production cycle, if improved profitability (euphemistically known as 'value-added') is to be achieved. This type of responsive, 'customer-centred' focus has been adapted to the language of architecture. Mass commodification is the new buzz-word to replace mass production. Nick Matthews, principal fellow of the engineering department at Warwick University, considers the Toyota prefabricated housing 'pod' system to be a 'primitive, rigid version' of his own Space 4 production model, which offers 'speed together with mass customisation'. Whereas Toyota deliver a fitted-out house module to site, Space 4 delivers flat-pack prefabricated panels ready for installation to minimise time-consuming wet-trades on site. The purchaser can get involved in the design and

production stages before the manufacturing of the panel system begins. In this way, and within reason, each house, although mass produced, can be customised on the conveyor belt.

Because economies of scale need to be maintained, consumer choice has its limits. Colour choices or simple add-ons, for example, are straightforward, so car manufacturers tend to supply variations of an easily adaptable theme on top of standard platforms. However, competition in this sector is forcing producers to offer a more meaningful range of choices. The powerful hold that the car manufacturing lobby has over its suppliers and workforce enables this to work effectively, although not necessarily to everyone's satisfaction. Expanding consumer choice will prove to be a more difficult task in the construction sector because of the industry's historically fragmented nature. Prefab housing, for example, is usually finished in 'traditional' brick skin and roof tiles. Future trends are barely addressed.

But is our new touchy-feely, built-in customer satisfaction attitude such a new thing? Production historian David Hounshell points out that 'flexible

The Interactive Automated Garage Door Pavilion was designed by Michael Jantzen in collaboration with the Human Research Shelter Institute to demonstrate that the most unexpected everyday materials and techniques can be put to good use in the creation of housing.

mass production meant that mass production as Ford had made it and defined it was, to all intents and purposes, dead by 1926'. In 1927 the Model T ceased production. Even more remarkably, the 1895 catalogue of Montgomery Ward included 56 varieties of clock targeted at distinct groups of potential buyers, and 131 different pocket knives, including 17 'for ladies'. Post-Fordism evidently pre-dated Henry Ford's first factory.

While Toyota's or Sekisui's modular industrialised housing units can be compared to Kurakawa's Nagakin Tower plug-ins of the mid-1970s, so Space 4, for example, is less futuristic than Buckminster Fuller's dreams for prefabrication. Both modern incarnations have better production standards than their earlier manifestations, but conceptually they have a lot in common. Housing Associations have for decades invited prospective tenants to choose door, kitchen and bathroom types from a catalogue. The bad news is that we haven't really progressed much further. The good news is that, at last, the logic of systems-built efficiencies is entering the mainstream market.

Fortunately, there are many exciting technologies – often related to state or university-funded research projects on products – which are finding their way into architectural solutions, but which probably would have seeped into the construction industry anyway. For example, as part of the broader energy efficiency challenge, fuel cell technology (which cannot be described as having been originated in the motor trade) is being incorporated into wireless office technology, providing clutter-free environments. Alternative energy sources which are being researched by NASA as well as the oil industry, for direct technology buy-in by the automotive sector, include flywheel technology and emission-free turbines which can easily transfer into construction products – local lighting sources or CHP (combined heat and power) systems, for example. A joint venture between Techtextil and BMW in Frankfurt is developing bioplastics – an alternative to glass-reinforced plastic (GRP) for car liners – made from natural materials.

Straw and hemp are already being processed into durable claddings, but could also be applied to low voltage circuit boards. These renewable materials will have applications across car manufacturing and construction.

The advances in 3-D modelling during the design process also transfers across industry. Although architects are less aware of its potential, this technology will increase its influence as computer and processing hardware becomes less expensive. Glass manufacture, use of computer animation, replaceable cladding panels and miniaturised electronics and security alarms are all part of the ongoing links between industry (of which car manufacture is a part) and construction. But the main technology transfers between cars and architecture – in the realm of ideas, more so than in practice – lie in the production techniques themselves.

Unlike previous generations, we now have a pervasive culture of restraint, characterised by the acknowledgement that we should 'respect nature's limits or pass up what technology promises', as Janine M.Benyus says in *Biomimicry: Innovation Inspired by Nature*, (1998). In Britain, we have both the Egan Report urging us to utilise automotive technological and managerial excellence, and Lord Rogers blaming the car for undermining the 'cohesive social structure of the city' in his book *Cities for a Small Planet*, (1998). While we continue to be faced with a situation whereby cities, and the buildings within them, are viewed as 'bad parasites' – from Herbert Girardet's *The Gaia Atlas of Cities*, (1998) – and the car is portrayed as a truly modern way of death, is it surprising that we have an ambivalent – some might say cowardly – attitude to the technology transference between the two? Early last century, Theo van Doesburg wrote that 'handicraft reduced men to the level of machines; the proper tendency for the machine (in the sense of cultural development) is as the unique medium of the very opposite, social liberation'. Regrettably, construction practices in the new millennium continue to prioritise a modern version of labour-intensive handicraft.

Smartslab, patented by B Consultants, is a new breed of building material. Not only are these durable aluminium and fibre-glass resin panels suitable for building walls, floors or ceilings, but full-colour light-emitting diodes are embedded in their surface. The construction method is borrowed from Formula 1 racing cars.

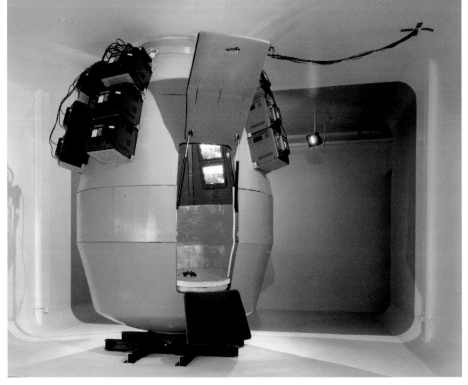

New York architects LOT/EK turn to discarded industrial equipment in their search for new spaces. A cement mixer's cylinder becomes a multimedia capsule (right), an oil container becomes a 'TV-Tank' with the addition of interior upholstery for maximum comfort (above). Top: The Morton Loft features a metal tube spanning the width of the space, transformed into a high-rise sleeping pod.

Made from an old shipping container, amongst other things, the Future Shack (2001) was designed by Sean Godsell Architects in Australia. As practical as it is stylish, this house for emergency and relief use can be mass-produced, is easy to transport and doesn't need foundations thanks to its very stable telescopic legs.

# BOYS AND THEIR TOYS

JONATHAN BELL

'The car has become an article of dress without which we feel uncertain, unclad and incomplete in the urban compound.'
Marshall McLuhan, *Understanding Media*, (1964)

Automotive culture has the power to transform buildings and environments, yet the most explicit manifestations of our urge to integrate, absorb and change are cars themselves. Custom car culture is steeped in mythology and legend, from its origins in pre-war America, when original thinkers like the late Ed 'Big Daddy' Roth melded and transcended the role of mechanic and coach-builder, bringing into being bizarre and unique creations. Roth took the fundamental, archaic forms of pre-war cars, combined them with elements from the race track, highly tuned engines and flamboyant paint jobs to create a form of motive surrealism.

'We're loading up our Woody with our boards inside.'
The Beach Boys, *Surfin' USA*, (1961)

The story of rock and roll's adoption of the automobile is well documented, allowing the crossover between car and counter-culture to lurch ever closer to the mainstream. Today, custom culture is just another facet of consumerism. British magazines like *Max Power, Fast Car, Revs* and *Cars and Car Conversions* make traditional lads mags look tame ('drive it like you stole it' reads a typical car sticker), with blatant exhortations to speed, cut up, grope and grind your way through life. These mooning loons in XR3is, whose Saturday nights are spent shredding low profile tyres in out of town car parks and deafening

each other with grossly over-powered stereos, are simply the manifestation of a generational desire to make the most of the car.

In *Driving Passion: The Psychology of the Car*, (1986), Peter Marsh and Peter Collett explain how the drive-in movie theatre catalysed the car's role as central to social activity; by removing behaviour previously confined to the living room to the car, the drive-in legitimised the car's social use, allowing for other auto-based activities to follow. The car's totemic role in the teenage

rite-of-passage has now remained unchanged for over half of century; only the style and level of display has changed.

Where once the downtown drag strips were rife with the sounds of chopped Model Ts, complete with dragster styling and bucket seats (see George Lucas's 1973 film *American Graffiti* for seminal scenes of teenage cruising), contemporary automotive night life is no less exotic. Cultures appropriate cars as a means of self-expression; witness the collision of Californian and Mexican car culture to create the lowrider, for example. Cars are lowered, cut, painted, sprayed, welded and re-assembled until each one is unique; an expression of a personality. Early lowriders favoured the '39 Chevy, stripped of its chrome ornaments to accentuate the car's sleek lines. Enthusiasts soon modified their rides with hydraulic systems – initially salvaged from de-commissioned B-52 bombers – as a means of instantly changing the ride height to placate an increasingly heavy-handed police force. Today, complex hydraulic systems allow suspensions to leap and dance, moving the display from purely visual to physical. Additionally, street racers are reclaiming, albeit aggressively, public space previously perceived as lost to the automobile's transitory effect. Public space was no longer the void between 'here' and 'there'; instead, it has become a zone in which to interact and exist.

At a more mainstream level, films like *Gone in 60 Seconds* and *The Fast and the Furious* are refreshed and updated for contemporary audiences, with period cars replaced with modern exotica (in the latter, the American muscle cars of the original movie have become outlandish Japanese supercars, an import market where upgrades and modifications are almost *de rigueur*). Cruising and street racing remains a fringe pursuit, from Tokyo to Washington, a pursuit that thrives on its sinister transgressive

image. Several Californian cities have resorted to passing anti-cruising laws, prohibiting the same vehicle from traversing the same stretch of road over and over again. Heaven help the lost tourist, yet what the authorities are really seeking to stamp out is an age-old mating ritual, a form of display that pre-dates motorised transport yet which continues to involve and adapt to its surroundings.

Not everyone can stretch to an expensive import to make a personal statement. Instead, mass culture tends to re-appropriate the everyday – the Escort, Golf, Astra – and transform them into symbols of transgression and display. In this world, the spoiler – a device initially devised to improve handling and stability at speed – becomes exaggerated and inflated. Instead of fulfilling some fundamental purpose, it has exploded into baroque expressionism, functioning as a kind of peacock-like display. Like lowriders before them, once-humble hatchbacks and saloons are elevated into an art form, pieces of mobile self-expression.

Today, specialist events like the Paris Tuning Show act as magnets for this subculture, a world where ads for alloy wheels blend into cheap pornography, where hi-fi installations are considered in great detail. Interiors, too, play a vital role in this world of ornamentation. Car stereo culture offers not only another means of self expression, but also allows the driver to control their surroundings, producing sounds so intense that the bystander is literally physically moved. All this is conveyed in an arcane language rich with power and mystery. 'Inside, a Pioneer P6000 CD head unit feeds an Alpine V12 amp, two 10-inch SPLX subs and a pair of Alpine DDDrive components.' *Max Power*, (2001).

Laying the groundwork for the cultural osmosis which integrates cars into society is rarely the preserve of the car companies. Yet through the medium of the limited

edition, the concept car and increasingly targeted marketing, manufacturers are striving to push their products towards the most profitable demographic. In an age of social responsibility, any sign that manufacturers are tempting transgression and anti-social behaviour is carefully monitored – advertising can no longer pander to the thrill of performance, speed is only invoked as a state which must be reduced and contained. Braking power, not brake horsepower, conveys the performance of the sports car.

Instead, concepts and niches arise, each carefully focus-grouped and targeted to ensure it makes a direct hit. These lifestyle vehicles are the mass market representation of custom. The small city car, and its pedal- and electric-powered relations, strive to break down the barrier erected between driver and pedestrian, reducing the automobile's weapon-like status, but also present a personable machine that pitches itself as an extension of character.

Contemporary culture remains infused by the automobile, a union that adapts and shifts to counter

any attempts at destabilisation. Motor industry downturns and currency crises matter little when the end project remains an object of desire and aspiration for millions. However we approach the automotive experience, either by distilling it into blandness or saturating our streets until automotion is oxymoronic, there'll remain a part of our hearts that is forever bewitched by the car.

Even when your car's not moving, it can still serve a social function – take the car boot sale, a social event uniquely shaped by automotive culture. Once a low-rent activity, the boot sale's essential simplicity – sellers fill their vehicles with unwanted goods and park them in a row to create instant shop fronts – has ensured its ubiquity. While desperation and poverty frequently stalk the rows of open tailgates, the majority of today's sales are highly organised, with long accepted rituals and rules for traders and buyers. Boot sales have also become the most adept exploiters of the impersonal architectural space contained within the car park, utilising the stacks and ramps as a transformable retail environment.

The new breed of cruisers embody teenage transgression, with the emphasis on crudity and illegal behaviour. Yet while the breast-baring, car-surfing and tyre-smoking contingency exists, magazines such as *Max Power* (strapline: 'the definitive guide to arsing about in cars') warn potential cruisees that this kind of high-jinks could get you fined and imprisoned. One suspects this is all part of the fun.

# 4. DESTINATION UNKNOWN

We've reached an impasse. Society is torn; economically bound to buy, use and maintain our cars, yet environmentally minded to cut back, hold off and conserve. Roads and cars generate ever stronger passions. Can these inherent conflicts be resolved?

The irony of modernist and post-modernist approaches to the car in the city is that they both sought the same outcome; cars functioning as a means of unencumbered, practical personal transport alongside the pedestrian. Right from the start, these intentions were confounded and confused. Modernist exhortations to leave the city via newly constructed roads and freeways were countered by an increase in traffic entering the city. The car's extended reach allowed the creation of suburbs – havens from the spectre of the city – but it also created the commuter's daily exodus between two sites of conflicting identity. These interrelated creations, the suburb and the commuter, have proved incompatible with the city and its existing architectural forms. Instead, we have towns of blank commuter boxes, devoid of focus and centre. These suburbs rely almost exclusively on the car; communities that stretch out, reaching for new land, more space and the empty promise of less traffic.

Carchitecture has been a long, slow evolutionary response to the problem of accommodating the inherent contradiction of the car; the car will set society free, an automotive society creates traffic, traffic enslaves society. In comparison, post-modern planning attempts to turn the clock back by creating spaces that function without the need for a car. The result is isolation. While pedestrianisation and New Urbanism can create successful pockets of authentically autophobic space, this community spirit is achieved through creating a sense of otherness, a segregation from the rest of society, denying the car's social function. Research by the Council for the Protection of Rural England shows that British commuting distances have increased by a third in the past decade. Americans already spend eight billion hours a year commuting .

At the heart of this futile flight is an overlooked truth: traffic has become the city's lifeblood. Like a shark, if a city stops moving, it will die: the movement of goods and people is fundamental to the function of the city. The analogy of roads to arteries and veins dates back to a mention in an engineering journal in 1890. Yet like blood, traffic can clot and choke; the city is often described in terms of the body; the lungs of a park, helping it breathe, the business district functioning as a heart. Traffic engineers devote themselves to the creation and maintenance of flow, ensuring that our progress is unhindered, a seamless fluid motion from node to node. Traffic is liquid, quickly spreading to fill every available space, seeping relentlessly into the 'increased capacity' of a new road scheme. In response, we build more roads, playing an endless game of catch-up that manifests itself in countrywide sprawl, a sea of asphalt and a state of siege between the car and society.

Is this all the car's fault? Not all anti-sprawlists are anti-car. Jane Jacobs' influential *The Death and Life of Great American Cities* (1961) was subtitled *The Failure of Town Planning*. Jacobs pointed out that although the automobile had bred cities with a random, decentralised sprawl, these conditions weren't necessarily entirely its fault. Jacobs argued that any form of mass transit would have resulted in the destruction of the compact, horse-powered city eulogised by planners and pedestrians alike. 'We went awry by replacing, in effect, each horse on the crowded city streets with half a dozen mechanized vehicles, instead of using each mechanized vehicle to replace half

NL Architects create projects that deliberately invert our standard response to car culture. Opposite: Parkhouse/ Carstadt makes the car park a dominant structure, a dramatic asphalt ribbon placed unashamedly in the city centre, the cars functioning as ornaments on its ramped surfaces. The practice describe themselves as autodidactic – educated in Delft, they lived in Amsterdam:

'Our recurrent fascination with mobility and tarmac perhaps could be traced back to being "educated" on the highway'.

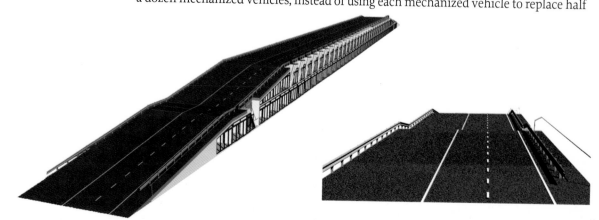

a dozen or so horses,' she claimed. Jacobs concluded that the automobile should work harder for its right to exist within the city – it should be used solely for transport, not as an extension of the means by which we live our lives. The exponential increase in horsepower since the era of the horse is a sign of greed, not need.

Here we stumble across another integral paradox; the idea that motorised transport should be allied solely to perceived needs is at odds with the realities of the market, the realities of our society and the ways in which we use our cars. When personal transport democratised our means of travelling around cities, it did so at the expense of jeopardising the many social functions the street fulfilled in the pre-auto age. Although the ways in which we use the car have evolved to replace these social functions, did we ruin our cities by shifting allegiance to the car? The 'square mile' of London's medieval city is not representative of the contemporary city as a whole. Instead, London's financial heart is directly at odds with the majority of Londoner's experience of their city – a compact space with low car use where people and buildings are dominant. The City is removed from contemporary notions of a 'city' – the car has inverted our perception of urbanism.

Charles Siegel's *Slow is Beautiful: Speed Limits as Political Decisions on Urban Form* charts the association between urban form and speed of travel. Siegel traces the evolution from the medieval 'walking city' through to the development of mass transit, starting with the horse-drawn omnibus through to the street car. As American suburbs developed, distance to amenities and work places increased as personal transport proliferated and improved, and the automobile developed its own set of spaces – the freeway, parking lot, off-ramp – gradually stretching the reach of the average person. It's the social and environmental consequences of this 'stretch' that lie at the heart of our response to carchitecture. Sprawl and pollution are the two over-riding problems for a future that continues to focus on cars without considering any alternative. We are urged to Reclaim the Streets, to Dump the Pump, to celebrate International Car-Free Day: anything, in short, that reverses our predilection for autophilia.

The historian Lewis Mumford believed that 'the right to have access to every building in the city by private motorcar in an age when everyone possesses such a vehicle is actually the right to destroy the city,' a prognosis confirmed by the great conurbations of the American West. Los Angeles' 1,187 square kilometres, criss-crossed by endless freeways and utterly impregnable to the pedestrian, is a disintegrated urbanism held together only by the glue of the car, the primary social facilitator. Ironically, the automobile wasn't directly responsible for the city's predilection to sprawl. From the early twentieth century, Henry Huntington's Big Red electric railcars pushed further and further out into the virgin desert, driven by revenue from oil dollars and the mighty irrigation projects that watered the new communities. Today, public transport is practically non-existent. Arguably, the city – in the pre-automotive sense of a dense, social space – has been destroyed, just as Mumford predicted. Yet Los Angeles exists, albeit dysfunctionally and unevenly, with Banham's paean to automobility – the fourth ecology – its unofficial manifesto.

In the traditional city, the dense European model that pre-dates mass wheeled transport by hundreds of years, the car is the enemy. Radical solutions to hasten integration have wrought destruction, creating a siege mentality. The

Nearly a century after the production line made its debut, Volkswagen is planning to reinvent the factory as entertainment. The Transparent Factory, currently under construction in Dresden, will build the forthcoming Volkswagen D1, a luxury vehicle targeted at Mercedes buyers. Instead of containing an automated production line, the factory will specialise in the high-quality assembly of pre-fabricated parts, a process made visible to passers-by through its large glass walls. Finished cars will be presented in a circular glass tower and buyers will be encouraged to visit the site to collect them. The complex is designed by Henn Architects, also responsible for VW's Autostadt.

**Shopping mall**
Until very recently, the only people interested in any analysis of the shopping mall and the out-of-town superstore tended to be academics specialising in urbanism. The rest of us were spending our time doing something altogether more fulfilling: shopping. And if you disagree with this, you are in a very insignificant minority. Thanks to the invention of the car and the refrigerator, shopping became the prime pastime of just about everyone. One phenomenon to come out of this retail revolution has perhaps not been the subject of serious academic study: the multi-pack. Now, with a car boot to fill, it is possible to bulk-buy bottled water by the supermarket-trolley load, and rolls of toilet paper come in convenient packs of twelve. With a freezer the size of a mortuary waiting at home in the double garage, a king-size tub of vanilla ice cream is difficult to resist. Shopping you can carry without mechanical means is becoming a rarity. In the United States, multi-packing has had inevitable results. Not only does every kitchen boast a cavernous refrigerator, designed to cope with one-gallon cartons of orange juice and family-sized vats of peanut butter, but obesity is now an epidemic, with breathtakingly huge pear shaped bodies to be seen waddling through every car park. No wonder American automobiles remain so large.

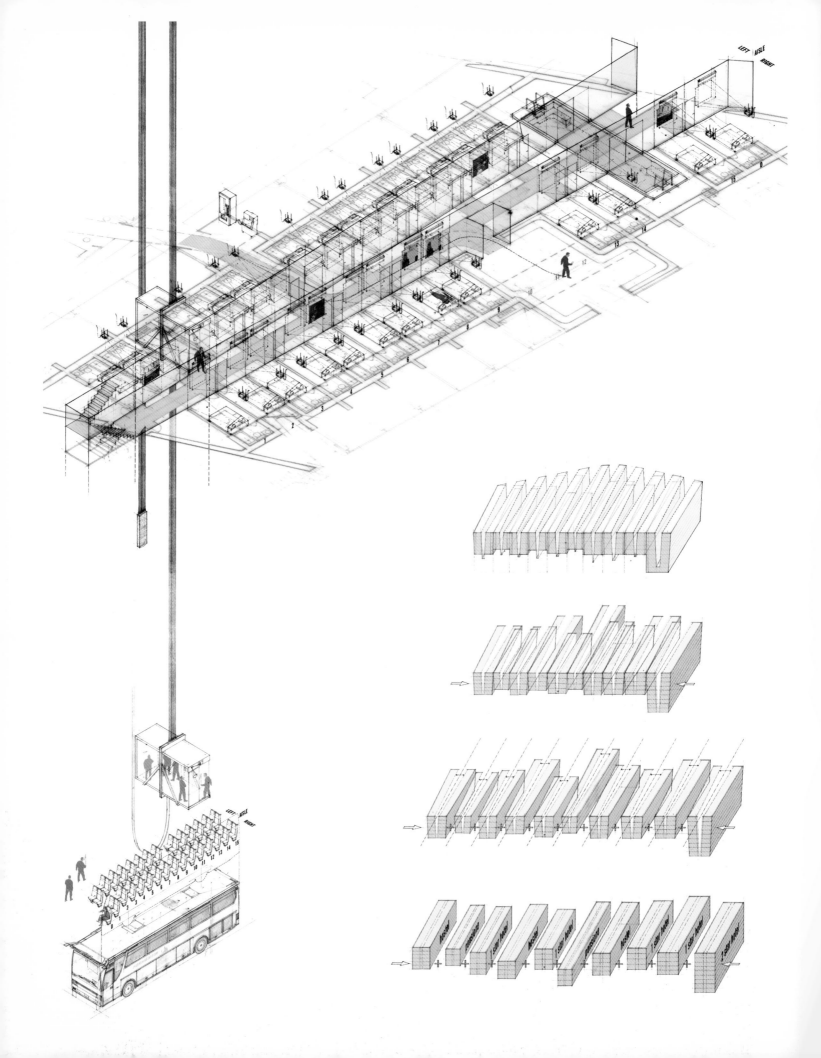

Opposite: The 'Tourbus Hotel' (2000) by architects Lewis.Tsurumaki.Lewis is a playful examination of the architectural space consumed by the average coach-load. Proposing a floor plan that exactly mirrors the configuration of the bus seats, tired and emotional day-trippers won't have too much trouble finding their room. Below: Taking a 'prototypical' suburban site, New Suburbanism (2000) offers a multi- layered environment, descending from linear house, complete with pool, down through the roof/lawn and garage to the cavernous isles of the 'Big Box' supermarket below.

megastructuralism of the grand modernist city plan, with its disregard for the individual and tacit approval of neo-fascist social policy, must never be repeated. Today, the billion-dollar transport plan must speak the language of inclusion, social responsibility and environmental sustainability – Boston's Big Dig, Britain's bypasses, the mighty Øresund Fixed Link that strides between Denmark and Sweden. These are projects billed as pragmatic long-term solutions; relief, not invigoration.

One solution to the integration (and perhaps ultimate dismantling) of auto-related infrastructure into the urban landscape is to stack. The multi-storey carpark, twin-tiered highway and vertical city – all draw on the automobile's ability for self-organising, using ramps and decks to sort, sift and store. Now long discredited – one only has to think of Britain's unloved brutalist monuments, Portsmouth's Tricorn Centre, Preston's Bus Station, Newcastle's main car park and Birmingham's Bull Ring, to see the opposition and hatred such architecture inspires. But the stack remains alive in architect's imaginations. Dutch architects Monolab and America's Lewis.Tsurumaki.Lewis, with their provocatively-titled New Suburbanism proposals, seek to relocate the stack, each having each identified the tracts of urban land that are otherwise blighted and ignored, their emptiness serving only to increase the sense of dislocation and distance between car and pedestrian. Monolab's schemes for Holland propose a series of 'Infrastructures', vast buildings which occupy the space above and around major transport interchanges, layering new function on areas otherwise notable for their absence of place, just cars speeding across the flat landscape.

These architectures of levels and stacks are strongly reminiscent of the megastructure – a semi-ironic reappraisal of an architectural language that extolled the machine age, mass production and all the values later shunned by the nano-level city planning of the New Urbanists. The megastructural ambitions of the 1960s and 1970s evoked a pedestrian/automobile utopia – with moving buildings, bridges and whole chunks of infrastructure to facilitate the creation of a car-based society. For the high-tech pioneers who believed in a synthesis of architecture and machine, the future would be dominated by developments of contemporary wonders like NASA's launcher crawler-tractor, built by the Marion Power Shovel Company from 1962–1965 to carry Saturn rockets from the Kennedy Space Center's vast Vertical Assembly Building across the Florida flatlands. Megastructures materialised, though not as sites of extreme urban density as originally envisaged. Instead, we have isolated concentrations of megastructural architecture – malls, new towns, interchanges – all acting as magnets to suck in and multiply traffic, far removed from high modernist megastructuralism.

New York-based firm Lewis.Tsurumaki.Lewis's New Suburbanism provides a light-hearted look at solving sprawl, by proposing that new neighbourhoods be constructed above the so-called 'Big Box' stores of America's infinite downtown. The Mall of America at Bloomington, Minnesota, typifies these environment. The size of 77 American football fields, the MoA (an apt, lumbering, flightless acronym) is the apogee of a style that began in the 1950s – out of town lots, unreachable to the pedestrian, and blanketed by a sea of cars. Despite general consensus that these behemoths of consumption suck the life from city centres, replacing the genuine social interaction stripped from the sidewalk by the car with a highly controlled atmosphere of faux-urbanism, the megastructural mall is still touted as central to (sub)urban renewal.

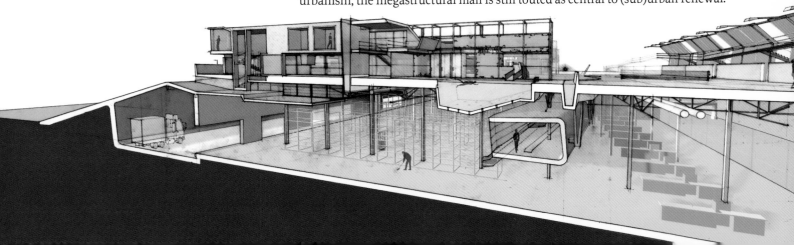

In Britain – at Gateshead, Bluewater, Lakeside – malls form miniature cities on the fringes of the greenbelt, complete with reproduction interior 'streets', 'plazas', 'boulevards' and food courts, patrolled by private security guards and surrounded by, you guessed it, car parks.

Our priorities are skewed. Today's true megastructures – huge, mobile communities – are about providing solace from the city, not a way of improving and encouraging urbanism. These escape strategies come in varying scales, from the 1,500 metre-long Freedom Ship, a planned 'city at sea' which uses technology to deny the existence of contemporary society, to the Recreational Vehicle, a roving, self-contained environment that simultaneously functions as architecture – home – while also providing an escape from architecture's unerring modernity. RV owners swarm and flock. Like that other icon of self-sufficiency, the Airstream, here is society masquerading as mass denial of urbanism; it's as if the suburbs upped and moved as one. Companies like Newell will build you vast, 15 metre-long mobile homes, complete with cantilevered, extending master bedrooms, double-glazing, deep pile carpets and other, uniquely American, comforts of home.

Now technology offers an escape, whether it's the digital distractions of the wired automobile, or the promise of auto-park systems. Automation was once the dream development of automotive interaction with the city, a push-button era that would make life swifter, smoother and safer. In the 1950s, the vision was the automated highway, a dream which clung to the concept of personal space while allowing for swift, hands-free inter-urban travel. The nuclear family could play chequers in their spacious, bubble-domed semi-automated cruise liner. GM's 1958 Firebird III concept car was an indication of things to come, designed to follow low-frequency power transmitted by cables embedded in the road. This wireless future remains just around the corner, although its supporters point out that a totally automated highway could carry three times the traffic than today's already congested roads. The flying car is another classic displacement technology, allowing one to escape the city in its entirety. In 1950s New Jersey, two Fly-in movie theatres were built, complete with airstrips and a special row for planes. Today, although practicality keeps our personal transport grounded, a devoted group of engineers keep the dream alive, literally flying in the face of planning convention.

For all our protestations about personal freedom, the possibility of abandoning our vehicle to a mechanised system that will store and return our vehicle, without the hassle of finding a parking space, is a more achievable urban dream. Companies such as Wöhr and Robotic Parking are staking their futures on vast, automated lots that make light work of racking up cars, saving time and space, the two most precious commodities at the start of the 21st century. Parking, in effect, has lost its financial lustre; the value of the derelict inner city sites stuffed with the expensive fruits of city bonuses can't compare with the returns on developing offices and housing.

Freedom remains an imperative. To drive is to be free, even if we are not actually moving. A means of reducing traffic while still maintaining the sense of individuality and control engendered by the car, is provided by Personal Rapid Transit (PRT). PRT has replaced the automated highway as the futurist vision of choice. Ostensibly a personal monorail, PRT systems would thread a network of slender tracks through a city, on which would operate small, electrically-powered vehicles with roughly the same

**Road markings**
Since Herbert Spencer's perceptive photographic study of road markings for *Typographica* magazine in the early 1960s, it has been impossible to view these street tattoos as anything other than the contemporary equivalent of cave paintings. Shapely patches of yellow or white paint (more recently blossoming into red, and even green), they are surely the symbols of humanity which will survive longest after the nuclear holocaust. And intriguing subjects they will make for analysis of the machine age: Look Left. Give Way. Stop. Arrows point straight ahead at every junction. Dotted white lines diverge into hatched areas which seem to forbid entry onto them. Yellow lines, single or double, define the gutter of every road. Curiously, removing the comfort zones created by the central white line actually slows traffic down – we are no longer so sure about our place on the road, wary of our own bulk and oncoming traffic. Zigzags, triangles, circles and squares: the road painter's art is to thread entire countries together, from end to end, in a great semiotic code waiting to be unstitched by the archaeologists of the future.

Above: The ULTra system melds personal transport with the monorail, using a sophisticated computer system to facilitate 'on demand' transport without congestion or over-crowding. Closely-spaced stations will allow passengers to pinpoint their destination, picking up empty cars and directing them to the closest stop. Each driverless, four-person unit can travel silently at speeds of up to 40kmh, running on a slender network of overhead tracks. Initially developed by the University of Bristol's Advanced Transport Group, a separate company, Advanced Transport Systems Ltd., has been established with the aim of building a pilot system in Cardiff in 2003. ULTra's acceptance will depend on a major shift in popular perception of the use of personal transport; each 'car' will in effect be a public space, commandeered for the duration of the journey and then returned to the public realm to be used again. Significantly, though, its proponents acknowledge that it will only complement existing methods of transport – widespread adoption is, for the moment, unlikely.

capacity as a private car. 'Off-line stations' would allow for unhindered progress to an exact destination without resorting to the stop-start progress of the train or the traffic, parking and pollution problems of the car. Paris and Hamburg developed, and abandoned, advanced working PRT prototypes, yet research continues. Raytheon's PRT 2000 project, the ULTra concept developed by Bristol University's Advanced Transport Group and a raft of other proposals, including Cincinatti's Skyloop and the Monomobile, a monorail complete with detachable light electric car, all promise a future of Maglev technology, elevated monorails and pollution free city-centres. This is a future where more movement within the city is to be stimulated – the habits created by the car will be fed, not discouraged.

In many respects, PRT is a throwback to early modernist visions, with cars and highways replaced by high-level monorails and electric pods. The rails and station infrastructure required by these proposals would exist in a curious intermediate space between public and private. Yet would more infrastructure 'free' our cities? Schemes to increase transport capacity rarely pass the verdict of hindsight. In the 1960s, highway engineer Robert Moses threaded fast expressways through Manhattan's vertical fabric, totally ignoring the call of public transport and blighting whole neighbourhoods. Moses went as far as specifying low bridges on his new freeways to keep trucks and buses away. Even at the time, Moses was seen as a pariah; had London's ringway system materialised in one piece, his British equivalent would doubtless carry the same stigma today.

For now, we must assume that our cities will be preserved, with all their anachronisms, one-way streets and social failings. While PRT and other, perhaps more fanciful, proposals might be lauded, funded and researched, their success ultimately depends on our willingness to re-shape our cities once more, raze, re-build, re-structure and adapt to the new environment. Any future transport system will have to be seamlessly integrated with current infrastructure; fundamental shifts that society will perhaps be unwilling to make.

Our problem is principally one of perception. Cars have evolved into social spaces, yet the car in the city rarely responds and interacts with pedestrians. Our architectural response to the car has been to reduce and restrain this social function, first by concentrating on flow and speed, then by imposing methods to restrict and control the way we use our cars. As a result, car-use is viewed as anti-social, sealed off from the world, unable to engage. Describing America's love/hate relationship with its interstate system as the result of an irreversible Faustian pact, documentary-maker Tom Lewis believes that Americans thrive on the individualist, isolated and sedentary lifestyle created by car dependence. In 1990, there were 115 million commuters in the US, of whom nearly 100 million used motorised private transport to get to work. Lewis quotes Marshall McLuhan, who believed that 'mass transportation is doomed to failure in North America, because a person's car is the only place where he can be alone and think.' Lewis continues, cataloguing how drivers have turned the road into extensions of their homes. 'Anyone who stands at the side of a really congested highway, say Interstate 405 in Los Angeles, will see drivers engaged in myriad activities – filing nails, talking on cellular telephones, grooming, picking noses, shaving, watching television, dressing, undressing or reading.' People have adapted to car-centric socialisation with remarkable adeptness.

What now? To be truly integrated with public transport and pedestrians, cars should not represent extensions of our homes, they should be extensions of the sidewalks. Cars have to be made more accountable – despite vast improvements in environmental efficiency and safety, the current situation is untenable. Key stretches of road, in America, Europe and the rest of the world, have reached saturation point, only now the traditional solution – building more, wider roads – is so widely discredited that it is no longer an option. Yet the paradox is that society believes, fundamentally, that it needs cars – to work and to live. In reality, governments need cars more, as politically expedient sources of revenue, not to mention convenient justifications for oil-centric foreign and domestic policies. A recent survey by Britain's Society of Motor Manufacturers and Traders revealed that in Britain, the typical family car will generate £50,000 of income – tax, maintenance, fuel, insurance, etc. – over an average lifespan of eight years, over five times its purchase cost, of which 20% is paid in road tax and petrol duty. Governments are unlikely to forsake this ready source, even for environmental reasons, in the foreseeable future.

Assume that car-use will increase, come hell or high taxation. Assume, too, that the trend towards more cosseting, isolated and ultimately pleasing mobile environments will continue; the motorist will become ever dislocated from society. In order to solve these two key problems – isolation and despoliation – we must plan more inclusive cities, urbanism that integrates rather than encourages further separation. For over a century, carchitecture has colluded with the automobile, facilitating expansion, sprawl and the unceasing vista of the asphalt nation. Instead, architecture and the automobile must learn to co-exist. This need not mean designing for door-to-door sprawl, aping the suburbs of the past, with their cul-de-sacs and acres of parking, not even the neotraditionalism of New Urbanism, with its emphasis on 'an airy, free-flowing interior enclosed within a colonial shell'. In an era of environmental accountability, the solution will also not lie in building more roads.

Today, the city dweller is faced with an almost Hobsonian choice; a sprawling city of many miles of choked freeways, with no discernible boundaries or centre, or a compact, dense, choked city, forever snarled with traffic and governed by technology and control systems. Carchitecture facilitated the sprawl, yet the latter was spawned by decades of misguided planning, half-baked solutions and ultimately contradictory policies. The political and social will to continue eviscerating our cities has evaporated, yet the flipside was a tendency to expand outwards, not upwards.

Suggestions as to how to entirely remove the car from our lives and from the city have gained currency in the past decade. J. H. Crawford's *Car-Free Cities* (2000), an impassioned plea for the wholescale rejection of personal motorised transport makes many valid points, including advocating an end to dedicated residential and business districts as a means of cutting down on commuting and journey times. But Crawford rejects key aspects of the contemporary city such as tall buildings and cites Venice as his key example of a successful car-free city, a freak of geography with a vast transient tourist population. His car-free city plans would have to be created from scratch, new towns whose construction and habitation would cause serious environmental imposition.

It's probable that there's no means of seamlessly integrating the automobile into our cities. Similarly, the dream of entirely car-free cities is also impossible. We're faced

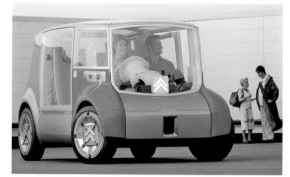

At the 2000 Paris Motor Show, Citroën showed the Osmose, a 'symbol of user-friendly vehicle design.' This boxy, four-square car was designed to 'initiate a new form of relations between pedestrians and motorists' and came with a radical social agenda – part taxi, part private car. Drivers would indicate their destination and willingness to take passengers, broadcasting availability to the WAP phone of potential passengers. The nearest suitable vehicle would be indicated to the 'guest', who can hop in to a special compartment at the rear.

Right: The CityCar project started in Martigny, Switzerland, in 1998, is intended to complement existing public transport. CityCars are designed to be housed in the 20 curved CityCar 'stations', designed by Nunatak Architects, where they can recharge their batteries and await their next journey. Anyone signed up for the scheme can simply hop in a spare car and drive away. The project uses a fleet of 30 Ligier Ambra two-seater micro cars, fitted with navigation equipment that allows a central control station to monitor each car's whereabouts. The CityCar project was preceded by the LEV (lightweight electric vehicle) initiative in Mendrisio. The small southern town, with 6,500 inhabitants, was given a large fleet of 'Light Vehicles', with the aim of getting 350 vehicles on the roads – 8% of the total car population – within four years. The target was easily achieved, thanks in part to the steady introduction of new electric vehicle technology during the late 1990s. Switzerland's home-grown LEV industry now includes the Twike (www.twike.ch), an electric three-wheeler. Schemes like these highlight the need for a combination of political and public willingness to assist alternative transport solutions.

with compromise, a strategy complicated by contradiction. Exhortations to use our cars less are accompanied by economic and social incentives to continue just as we were. The current state of futurism is hardly encouraging – a personal monorail will face a strong challenge from the latest air-conditioned, fully-wired, highly-styled product of the world's car makers. Carchitecture has moved on from its role as explicit advocate of motorised cities, replete with high-speed freeways, parking for all and not a particle of pollution. Instead, it has become a subtler architecture of persuasion and promotion, ensuring the continuation of a complex system of interdependent relationships: cars, people, governments, corporations.

The megastructural visions, vast engineering projects, motorway intersections, car parks and off-ramps, remain the purest expressions of carchitecture. Today auto-centric design has shifted from architecture to the car itself, not only the most technologically advanced possession we own, but also the most highly styled item. Cars are the most accessible 'design' object most people ever see. Incremental changes and new models define our environment and shape the way we see and perceive the future, far more so than the visions provided by architects. The carchitecture of the future will be the environments we drive, not the environments we drive through. At the heart of the relationship between architecture and cars is the capacity to adapt, a two-way process that confounds demand for swift and certain change. We can complain, legislate, debate and lament all we like, yet only be certain of one thing; carchitecture might mutate, switch allegiance, form and function, but ultimately it remains an irreversible state of mind.

'The city has the ability to recreate itself silently and invisibly, as if it were truly a living thing.'
Peter Ackroyd, *London, the Biography of a City*, (2000)

## Pedestrianised zones

The pedestrian precinct is carchitecture at its most rarefied, a phenomenon of the late 20th century that owes its very existence to the automobile yet is defined by the car's complete absence. Urban traffic is not a recent invention, but no one felt the need to create such protective total-exclusion zones when the city's streets were teeming with horse-drawn vehicles, riders and overloaded handcarts. It's not even as if pedestrians don't have their own designated zone, in theory at any rate: the pavement. Admittedly, this space can get rather crowded, as pedestrians increasingly find themselves having to share their domain with timid cyclists unwilling to risk their luck on the road, not to mention the more brazen ones who consider the pavement a useful additional lane, to be swerved into and out of at will. Then there is the proliferation of rollerbladers, skateboarders and scooter-riders to contend with, wheeled forms of transport that don't fit into any existing category of road user. But the answer to the oversubscription of city pavements does not necessarily lie in the pedestrianised zone: far from being designed with the needs of the wheel-free urbanite in mind, these developments tend to be driven by purely commercial motives. What is a pedestrianised zone if not a badly-planned shopping mall, one that doesn't even offer the benefits of shelter from the elements, generous toilet facilities and ample parking? After dark, when the shops are shut, these artificial environments seem strangely devoid of purpose. Deserted by shoppers and without traffic to inject some much-needed action, they can become sinister and threatening, avoided by all but the very brave. No wonder these spaces are rife for after-hours colonisation by skateboarders keen to incorporate the street furniture into their latest moves.

Photography credits:

Cover: courtesy of Alex de Rijke
p.2-3: 'Baltimore, Parking Lot for Orioles Game, 1996', © Alex S. MacLean/landslides
p.4-5: 'Gaithersburg, Cul-de-sac Subdivision, 2001', © Alex S. MacLean/landslides
p.6-7: 'Atlanta, Highway Interchange Knot, 2001', © Alex S. MacLean/landslides
p.8-9: courtesy of Fiat
p.10: VW Autostadt, photo by Elisabeth Scheder-Bieschin
p.12-13: courtesy of Fiat
p.14: courtesy of Volkswagen
p.17: photos by Alex De Rijke
p.18-19: courtesy of BMW
p.20: courtesy of Fiat
p.21 top: courtesy of Renault
p.21 bottom left: courtesy of Renault
p.21 bottom right: courtesy of Fiat
p.22 top: courtesy of VW
p.22 bottom: courtesy of I-DE-A Institute
p.23: courtesy of Nissan
p.24-29: photos by Andrew Cross
p.33: courtesy of Steven Brower
p.34 right, p.35 bottom: photos by J.D. Merriweather, courtesy of Wilsonart and Inside Design
p.37: courtesy of General Motors
p.38-39 bottom: courtesy of The Newell Coach Company
p.39 top: photos by Valerio Castelli, courtesy of Bellini Archivio
p.41: photos by Inga Knölke, courtesy of Martí Guixé
p.42-43: photos © Philippe Ruault, courtesy Manuelle Gautrand Architects.
p.44-45: courtesy of Odile Decq and Benoît Cornette Architects
p.46: courtesy of Steinmann & Schmid
p.47-49: photos © Christian Richters, courtesy of Neutelings Riedijk Architects
p.50-51: photos by Yorick Carroux © the designers/Drive-In
p.55 © Fondation Le Corbusier, Paris/DACS, London 2001
p.56: © Marc Newson
p.57 top: © Marc Newson
p.57 bottom: courtesy of Ford
p.58 top: courtesy of VW
p.58 bottom: courtesy of Ford
p.59 bottom right: courtesy of DaimlerChrysler
p.59 top left: courtesy of DaimlerChrysler
p.60 bottom left: courtesy of Audi
p.60 right: courtesy of MCC
p.64 courtesy of Enrico Tedeschi
p.65 top: courtesy of Airboard Industries Limited
p.65 bottom left and right: courtesy of Moller International, Inc.
p.66-67: Breathaliser and speed camera photos by Nigel Jackson
p.68: photos by Alex De Rijke
p.70 top: courtesy of Sandy McCreery
p.70 bottom: © FLC/ADAGP, Paris and DACS, London 2001
p.71: courtesy of Sandy McCreery
p.73: photo by Anne Odling-Smee
p.74: photo by Jason Oddy
p.75: courtesy of Sandy McCreery
p.76-77: photo by Dan Holdsworth
p.79-81, p.82 top: photos by Adrian Fisk
p.82 bottom: © Justin Leighton/Network
p.85: courtesy of Solent News and Picture Agency
p.86 top: photo by Alex De Rijke
p.86 bottom: © Newcastle Chronicle and Journal
p.88-89: photo © Tomoko Yoneda
p.94-95: courtesy of Robotic Parking, Inc.
p.96: photos by Chris Gascoigne, courtesy of CZWG Architects
p.100: photo by Elisabeth Scheder-Bieschin
p.101: Courtesy of VW Autostadt
p.102: photo by Elisabeth Scheder-Bieschin
p.103 left: photo by Elisabeth Scheder-Bieschin
p.103 top and bottom right: courtesy of Audi
p.104: courtesy of Otto Wöhr GmbH
p.105 top: courtesy of BMW
p.105 left: courtesy of Otto Wöhr GmbH
p.105 right: courtesy of MCC
p.106: courtesy of VW
p.108 top: courtesy of B Consultants
p.108 bottom left: ©Arch. Alessandro Laterza, Via De Cristoforis, 10 21100, Varese, Italy, alessandro.laterza@tin.it
p.108 bottom right: courtesy of Cartwright Pickard Architects
p.109: photo by Jeremy Young, courtesy of BDP
p.110: © Michael Jantzen
p.111: courtesy of B Consultants
p.112: © Paul Warchol Photography Inc.
p.113: courtesy of Sean Godsell Architects
p.114-115: photos by Andrew Tipping
p.116-117: Parking meter, photo by Nigel Jackson
p.118-119: © NL Architects
p.121: courtesy of VW
p.122-123: © Lewis.Tsurumaki.Lewis
p.124: © ULTra, courtesy of Richard Teychenne (www.atsltd.co.uk)
p.125: photo by George A. Cretton
p.126: courtesy of Citroën


Further Reading

1. MIRROR, SIGNAL, MANOEUVRE
– Autoland: Pictures from Switzerland, Nicolas Faure, Scalo Press, 1999
– The Automobile Age, James Flink, MIT Press, 1990
– The Car Culture, James Flink, MIT Press, 1975
– The Car and the City: The Automobile, the Built Environment, and Daily Urban Life, Martin Wachs and Margaret Crawford, University of Michigan Press, 1992
– The Car Makers, Graham Turner, Pelican Books, 1964
– Down the Asphalt Path: The Automobile and the American City, Clay McShane, Columbia University Press, 1994
– How to design a Petrol Station, Marcello Minale, Booth-Clibborn Editions, 2000
– The New City, edited by Donald Canty, Urban America Inc., 1969
– Taking the Wheel: Women and the Coming of the Motor Age, Virginia Scharff, University of New Mexico Press, 1992
– Towards a New Architecture, Le Corbusier, Architectural Press, 1946

2. THE FUELLING OF DESIRE
– AS in DS: An Eye on the Road, Alison Smithson, Delft University Press, 1983
– Automobiles by Architects, Ivan Margolius, Academy Editions, 2000
– Brightwork: Class American Car Ornamentation, Ken Steacy, Chronicle Books, 2000
– Building the New World: Studies in the Modern Architecture of Latin America 1930-1960, Valerie Fraser, Verso, 2001
– City Center to Regional Mall: Architecture, the Automobile, and Retailing in Los Angeles, 1920-1950, Richard Longstreth, MIT Press, 1998
– City of Quartz: Excavating the Future in Los Angeles, Mike Davis, Pimlico, 1998
– Exquisite Corpse, Michael Sorkin, Verso, 1994
– The Drive-In, the Supermarket, and the Transformation of Commercial Space in Los Angeles, 1914-1941, Richard W. Longstreth, MIT Press, 2000
– Fast Food: Roadside Restaurants in the Automobile Age, John A.Jakle, Keith A.Sculle, John Hopkins University Press, 1999
– "Fill 'er Up" An Architectural History of America's Gas Stations, Daniel Vieyra, Collier Macmillan, 1979
– Freeways, Lawrence Halperin, Reinhold Publishing, 1966
– Industry, Architecture and Engineering: American Ingenuity 1750 - 1950, Louis Bergeron, Maria Teresa Maiullari-Pontois, Abrams Books, 2000
– Los Angeles: The Architecture of Four Ecologies, Reyner Banham, Penguin, 1971
– Los Angeles: The City Observed, Charles Moore, Peter Becker and Regula Campbell, Vintage Books, 1984
– Main Street to Miracle Mile: American Roadside Architecture, Chester H. Liebs, John Hopkins University Press, 1995
– Megastructures: Urban Futures of the Recent Past, Reyner Banham, Thames and Hudson, 1976
– The Motel in America, John A.Jakle, Keith A.Sculle and Jefferson S.Rogers, John Hopkins University Press, 1996
– Motopia: A Study in the Evolution of Urban Landscape, Geoffrey Jellicoe, Studio Books, 1961
– Moving Objects: 30 Years of Vehicle Design at the Royal College of Art, edited by Stephen Bayley and Giles Chapman, Eye-Q, 1999
– On the Road: the art of engineering in the car age, edited by Catherine Croft, Architecture Foundation, 1999
– Populuxe, Thomas Hine, Bloomsbury, 1987
– Seaside, Steven Brooke, Pelican Publishing, 1995
– Strangely Familiar: Narratives of Architecture in the City, Iain Borden et al, Routledge, 1998
– Streamlined: A Metaphor for Progress, edited by Claude Lichtenstein and Franz Engler, Lars Müller Publishers, 1996

3. DRIVEN TO DISTRACTION
– Asphalt Nation: How The Automobile Took Over America and How We Can Take It Back, Jane Holtz Kay, University of California Press, 1998
– Autogeddon, Heathcote Williams, Jonathan Cape, 1991
– Customized: Art Inspired by Hot Rods, Low Riders and American Car Culture, edited by Nora Donnelly, Harry N.Abrams, 2000
– The Death and Life of Great American Cities, Jane Jacobs, Vantage Books, 1961
– Divided Highways: Building the Interstate Highways, Transforming American Life, Tom Lewis, Penguin, 1999
– The Ecology of the Automobile, Peter Freund and George Martin, Black Rose Books, 2000
– The Geography of Nowhere: The Rise and Decline of America's Man-Made Landscape, James Howard Kunstler, Touchstone Books, 1994
– Leadville: A Biography of the A40, Edward Platt, Picador, 2000
– I Love Fast Cars, Craig McDean, powerHouse Books, 1999
– The 100 Mile City, Deyan Sudjic, Andre Deutsch, 1992
– Park and Ride, Miranda Sawyer, Abacus, 2000
– Sex, drink and fast cars, Stephen Bayley, Faber and Faber, 1986
– Speed: Visions of an Accelerated Age, edited by Jeremy Millar and Michiel Schwarz, Photographer's Gallery/Whitechapel, 1998
– Suburban Nation : The Rise of Sprawl and the Decline of the American Dream, Andres Duany, Elizabeth Plater-Zyberk, Jeff Speck, North Point Press, 2001

4. DESTINATION UNKNOWN
– Carfree Cities, J.H. Crawford, Paul & Co. Publishing, 2000
– Cities for a Small Planet, Richard Rogers, Faber & Faber, 1997
– The City After the Automobile: An Architect's Vision, Moshe Safdie, Basic Books, 1997
– Divorce Your Car! Ending the Love Affair With the Automobile, Katie Alvord, Stephanie Mills, Katharine T.Alvord, New Society Publishers, 2000
– Driving Passion: The Pyschology of the Car, Peter Marsh and Peter Collett, Jonathan Cape, 1986
– The End of the Road: From World Car Crisis to Sustainable Transportation, Wolfgang Zuckermann, Chelsea Green Publishing, 1991
– The Future of London, Edward Carter, Pelican Books, 1962
– Home From Nowhere: Remaking Our Everyday World For the 21st Century, James Howard Kunstler, Touchstone Books, 1998
– London 2000, Peter Hall, Faber, 1971
– Motorways in London, J.Michael Thomson, Gerald Duckworth, 1969
– A New London, Richard Rogers and Mark Fisher, Penguin, 1992
– The Next American Metropolis: Ecology, Community, and the American Dream, Peter Calthorpe, Princeton Architectural Press, 1993
– Street Reclaiming: Creating Livable Streets and Vibrant Communities, David Engwicht, New Society Publishers, 1999
– Sustainability and Cities: Overcoming Automobile Dependence, Peter Newman & Jeff Kenworthy, Island Press, 1999
– <yellow> Rhythms: A Roundabout for London, Eyal Weizman, 010 Publishers, 2000


see www.carchitecture.net for links